Praise For Guit

A Stellar Writing

"The Guitar Head books have been an invaluable resource, helping me fulfill a lifetime dream of mastering guitar soloing. It's my retirement plan! Keep the books coming, as I just can't get enough! Thank you so much for your stellar writing and loving approach to the guitar — it really resonates with me."

- *Stephen E. Dannenbaum*

50's Mid-Life Guitar Start up

"Starting up guitar for myself in my late 50's after sending all my kids thru guitar school, Really great books, I have purchased them all. Very helpful to fill in the blanks. Easy to follow and I really enjoy his writing style and humor"

- *Wayne Humphrey*

Exceeded Expectations

"Guitar fretboard is the first book I bought from Guitar Head. I purchased this book with much skepticism. However my skepticism quickly went away. I am an online student with Berklee College of Music and can tell you their books are real deal. Looking forward to purchasing the complete series of books from Guitar Head."

- *Steven Retalic*

Great hints and tips

"Guitar Head allowed me to view the fretboard entirely differently than I have for over 50 YEARS! Thank You Guitar Head!"

- *Kim Gregg*

GUITAR CHORDS
FOR
BEGINNERS

A **14 - Day Program** To Master
Chord Shifts, Strumming & Longer Progression
To Nail Your **Favourite Songs**

GUITAR HEAD

✉ gh@theguitarhead.com

Ⓞ ⓕ /theguitarhead

Disclaimer

Dedication

*We dedicate this book to the complete
Guitar Head team,
supporters, well-wishers and
the Guitar Head community.*

*It goes without saying that we
would not have gotten
this far without
your encouragement,
critique and support*

Table Of Contents

Free Guitar Head Bonuses

Audio Files

All Guitar Head books come with audio tracks for the licks inside the book. These audio tracks are an integral part of the book - they ensure you are playing the charts and chords the way they are intended to be played.

Lifetime access to Guitar Head Community

Being around like-minded people is the first step to being successful at anything. The Guitar Head community is a place where you can find people who are willing to listen to your music, answer your questions or talk anything guitar.

Email Newsletters Sent Directly to Your Inbox

We send regular guitar lessons and tips to all our subscribers. Our subscribers are also the first to know about Guitar Head giveaways and holiday discounts.

Free PDF

Guitar mastery is all about the details! Getting the small things right and avoiding mistakes that can slow your guitar journey by years. So, we wrote a book about 25 of the most common mistakes guitarists make and decided to give it for free to all Guitar Head readers.

You can grab a copy of the free book, the audio files and subscribe to the newsletter by following the link below.

All these bonuses are a 100% free, with no strings attached. You won't need to enter any personal details other than your first name and email address.

To get your bonuses, go to: ***www.theguitarhead.com/bonus***

INTRODUCTION

Hey there! Thanks for joining us, and welcome to the first step in your magical music journey.

During the next 14 days, you'll acquire enough knowledge and know-how to play the songs you love the most, create your own music, and most importantly, identify most chords in Western music.

Yes, we're going to go through the basics together, and I will give you all the tools you need to build your guitar knowledge with solid foundations that will last for a lifetime.

But hey, this is getting too serious; we'll also have obnoxious amounts of fun, go through absolute classics, and crack a laugh or two.

Moreover, let me tell you that this is a book written with the passion and love three decades of professional guitar playing have given me, so it will very likely spark that in you as well. Furthermore, I promise that by the end of this book, you'll be able to play with other musicians, create tunes, and understand the guitar like never before.

While this book has been designed to be completed in 14 days, feel free to take a day off if you need to. Don't be hard on yourself trying to one-shot the program without breaks.

That being said, this is a practical guide to guitar-chord proficiency. Although we will address theory and important concepts, you'll be playing a lot every day.

Finally, consider this a manual on magic.

Indeed, creating music is making magic, and here you will learn all the magician tricks these years on the road have given me. I'll pass on the information and responsibility to you, and with enough practice; you'll be making magic in less than a month.

So, I hope you're ready to become a better guitarist and walk the long and winding road of the musician. You'll see that, when you fret a chord properly and caress the strings, you'll be transported along with those around you into the realm of music that you haven't experienced before.

Yes, it's as easy as that. Sometimes, it feels like magic, and somehow, it is.

Are you ready to make dreams come true?

Buckle up ! This journey starts right now!

PART 1

YOUR FIRST 14 DAYS

═ CHAPTER 1 ═

FIRST STEPS

Getting to Know Your Instrument

In the following two weeks, you're going to learn and play so much that your guitar might be the thing you hold the most. Therefore, we need to learn how to comfortably play it.

Remember, what you have in your hands is an infinite canvas for creation, your new best friend.

But let's begin from scratch so you can build all your guitar knowledge on solid ground with nothing but rock-hard bricks of professional tips and exciting techniques.

The guitar is, by default, a 6-string instrument. Of course, you can now find them with 7 and 8 strings or you can talk to Uncle Keith (Richards) who wrote countless hits on a 5-string guitar. That being said, we are always going to talk about a 6-string guitar in this book.

Talking about strings, these will increase their thickness as we move up from the 1st string (the thinnest) to the 6th string (the thickest). Each of these strings is tuned to a specific note; the thinner the string, the higher the pitch.

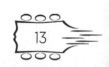

These six strings go from the bridge all the way to the top of the guitar where they are wrapped around the tuners. Turning the tuners helps you to tune the guitar since they make the strings more or less tense. The combination of tension and size gives you every note.

There are many different types of guitars; these are the most important three:

» **Acoustic guitars:** These guitars usually have a soundhole and are built to generate sound on their own without being plugged into any other source. Usually, they have a wooden bridge, a big, wide body for resonance, and either bronze or nylon strings.

» **Acoustic-electric guitars:** These guitars are the same as the above with the addition of a pickup system to translate the vibration of every string into a current that is then turned into sound. These guitars usually have volume and tone knobs and some come with a built-in tuner.

» **Electric guitars:** Electric guitars are by far the most abundant. Most feature a solid body, some a semi-hollow body, and fewer a hollow body. Electric guitars feature pickups that translate sound vibration into sound that can be amplified. They usually have multiple knobs and toggles to fine-tune the sounds coming from them.

Your First Day with the Guitar!

As we said earlier, we're going to learn the guitar from absolute scratch. Therefore, we are going to spend a lot of time having fun and learning with our new instrument. In order not to develop bad habits and enjoy playing with a good posture, let's learn the basics about how to hold and play the guitar.

How Do I Hold My Guitar?

Guitar players can be divided into two big groups: those who play standing and those who play sitting down. We are going to be in the second group since it is much easier to learn. That being said, by the moment you finish this book, you'll be able to demonstrate your talent sitting, standing, or dancing like mad on the stage.

So, if you are right-handed, place the waist of the guitar (the narrowest part of the body) over your right leg. If you are left-handed, you can place your guitar on your left leg. Now, let it sit with the neck parallel to the floor (completely horizontal) and hold it close to your chest and stomach.

Also, make sure that your back is completely straight. This is very important so you don't develop any bad habits that are difficult to get rid of later on. You can still look and hear your guitar, but try not to bend over it. Otherwise, your lower and upper back will start to hurt after a little time. Plus, you won't look as amazing when your pictures land on the cover of the hottest magazines on the planet.

Finally, try to avoid rolling the guitar neck up to see where your fingers are. This is not because of aesthetics but because that movement can create unnecessary tension in your wrist, making playing harder instead of simpler.

Don't worry, though, it is OK to do it at the beginning a little but try to avoid it as much as possible.

The Position of My Picking Hand

As you noticed that the guitar "waist" was designed to help you play more comfortably. Well, the upper part of the guitar (where the body is at its widest) is the perfect place to rest your picking hand's arm. This way, you have enough space to strum easily over the sound hole.

When talking about electric guitars which usually don't feature such a huge body you'll realize your elbow can rest on the front of the guitar rather than on top. Other than that, the premise is the same, to play between the bridge and the beginning of the neck.

Holding the Pick

Your index finger and your thumb will be responsible for holding your pick. The perfect way to do it is by stretching your index finger and placing the pick over the last

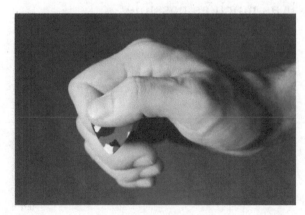

phalanx with the tip looking down, toward the nail. Once you've done that, put the thumb on top and make sure you have a strong enough grip to avoid dropping it but loose enough to have maneuverability.

> **PRO TIP:** Picks vary in thickness and shape. For strumming chords and learning how to play, stay away from picks thicker than 1 millimeter. Ideally, you should stay within .74 and 1mm. Finally, some picks offer a grip on the side; those are better when starting out and to avoid picks dropping from sweaty fingers.

The Position of My Fretting Hand

As soon as you put your hand to the guitar neck, you'll realize that it will naturally create a "C" shape with it, and the neck will sit exactly inside of it. Now, move your thumb down and your fingers will move "out" of the fretboard naturally as well.

This position will allow you to have more strength in your hand without doing any additional effort. Those who have bigger hands will find their thumb sticks out of the fretboard. This is not at all a problem; in fact, with time and practice, you can use it to your advantage (it's the secret 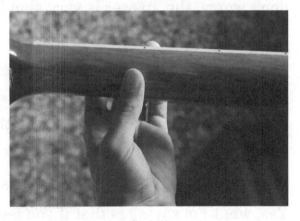 move of Jimi Hendrix and John Mayer among many others).

Smaller hands, on the other hand, will find that lowering the thumb makes the position more comfortable.

> **PRO TIP:** The secret to mastering your fretting hand is utilizing the muscles between the thumb and the index finger to press strings. Strength is not in your fingers but in your hand; therefore, placing it correctly is paramount to playing better.

Fretting the Notes on My Guitar

By fretting notes on a guitar, we can change their pitch. You might have noticed some metal bars on your fretboard. These are called frets and are a 20th-century innovation to divide the fretboard into every note you can play. Thus, every time you fret a string and play it, you'll be playing a different note. Depending on what note or notes you fret, you'll get a note or a series of notes we call chords.

"But wait, not so fast. How in the world do I "fret" a string?" If you're wondering about this and using your pick to scratch the top of your head, don't worry, the answer is very simple: you have to press the strings down with your fingers.

Speaking of pressing the strings, what part of the finger do I use to press on the strings? Well, the answer to that question is the tip of your fingers. This is not our random occurrence; it is the part of the finger that has enough meat to be even when pressed with a bone behind to keep it strong.

With time, you'll have callouses in the tips that will make everything easier. Yes, what I'm saying is that if you feel a little pain at the beginning there's nothing to worry about, just stop until it goes away and then start over. Before you know it, it'll be gone for good.

Remember that the strength is not in the fingers but in the hand muscles. Therefore, if you find yourself making too much pressure to get a good sound, you have to revise the position of your hand rather than applying more pressure with your fingers.

What if I get a Buzzy Sound?

If you get a buzzy sound with your guitar don't freak out, it's completely normal. We've all gone through that at the beginning; even the biggest guitar icon you can think of went through that moment.

But where does that annoying sound come from?

» Your string is buzzing because you're not applying enough pressure using your hands' muscles.

» You might also be placing your finger too far away from the fret of the note you want to play.

» You are placing your finger on top of the fret of the note you want to play.

Once you've corrected your fretting hand, you'll very likely be able to fix the buzzing.

In this sample picture, you can see how to correctly fret the second note of the 6th string. Notice how the finger is close to the fret without touching it.

In the image below, the finger is pressing down far from the fret. This is bad fretting.

PRO TIP: Short nails on your fretting hand will always make it easier to play while longer nails might work as a pick replacement for your picking hand. Trying to fret notes with long nails can be a recipe for disaster since they can scratch your fingerboard and make strings buzz.

Let's awaken your fingers

While playing chords on guitar is not a difficult thing, we have to make our muscles stronger and work on fine-tuning our coordination to make sure all movements flow smoothly, feel effortless, and, above all, we feel no pain.

To help us on our way to that goal, we're going to go through a series of very simple exercises that might be complicated until you play them daily and get to master them. You can think of this part of the book as the foundational stone to your sonic empire; the first step in mastering the instrument.

Finally, they are great to warm up, and doing them every time you pick up the guitar will help you a lot.

Exercise 1 – Coordination

Let's start by playing each string in an "open" position. That is, without fretting with our left hand. Use only your right hand to play each string with the pick. It's ok if you don't pluck the correct string every time - getting it right is hard at first! Take your time and try as many times as you need.

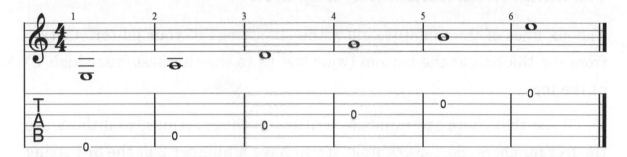

> Check out the audio track in the bonus section to see how the
> exercise sounds.

How to read the TAB?

Oh my God! You're absolutely right! We were so enthusiastic about awakening those fingers that I didn't explain how to read the tab you have in front of you. I'm sorry; I promise you it won't happen again.

Let's go right into it. Let me say that you're going to be using tablatures not only for this book but probably your entire playing life.

What is a Tablature?

A tablature is an alternative to learning how to read music. Moreover, we could think of it as a shortcut straight to playing written music without learning the theory behind traditional music notation.

Don't get me wrong, I'm not saying you shouldn't learn to read music, I'm saying that you don't need to; at least at the beginning.

So, to begin with, you could think of a tablature as a map of the guitar neck showing you the strings and what frets to place your fingers at. That being said, a tablature will not give you any rhythm notation but we'll take care of that later on in this book.

The Guitar Neck, Horizontally Displayed

The six lines of the tablature show the six strings of your guitar starting from the thickest at the bottom (your low E) to the thinnest (your high E) at the top.

You'll see that there are numbers written on those strings, well those are the fret numbers. So, for example, if you have a number 2 at the 3rd string (the third from the top), you'll play the 3rd string fretted at the 2nd fret.

Likewise, if you have the number 2 followed by a 4 on the same string, you'll play the same string at the 4th fret.

What happens if you encounter a zero (0)? Well, your zero fret is the open string so you have to just play the string without fretting it anywhere.

Let's put this all together in a very famous example:

You don't have to pay attention (for now) to the upper part since we'll take care of rhythm patterns later on in this book.

So, the way to read that tablature is the following:

» Play the 4th string at the 2nd fret twice

» Play the 4th string at the 4th fret

» Play the 4th string at the 2nd fret

» Play the 3rd string at the 2nd fret

» Play the 3rd string at the 1st fret

Could you play the sequence? Did it ring a bell? Well, yeah, it is the happy birthday song. Now you can be the champion uncle at your nephew's party!

Tablatures or tabs don't show finger numbers but they show fret numbers. So, when you're reading a tab like the one above you can use the finger that feels the most comfortable to you for that specific movement. As a rule of thumb, you can use the index finger for the 1st fret, the middle finger for the 2nd fret, the ring finger for the 3rd fret, and the pinky for the 4th fret. You can move this same structure from the starting fret to the last one you need to play.

OK, now that we're clear about what a tablature is, let's keep moving so you can master your instrument one cool exercise at a time.

Exercise 2 – Coordination & Strength

Now use your index finger on the 2nd fret every second note. Try to pluck the string as soon as you put your finger down. Remember to place the finger close to the fret but not on top.

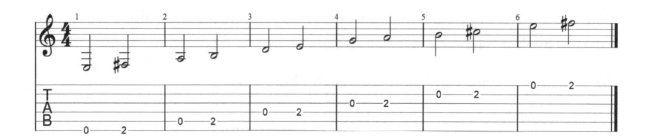

Congratulations and welcome to day two! If your fingers are ready for some more action, we're going to build some Arnold Schwarzenegger-esque strength to them. Furthermore, today you'll get to use all your fingers on the fretboard to have more fun.

PRO TIP: The exercises we'll see today aren't about speed or perfection; you need to focus on having no buzzing sounds and playing the right string with your picking hand. Those are your goals; we'll work on speed later on.

Exercise 3 – Coordination & Strength with Three Fingers

Let's add the ring finger. This time, place your index finger on the 1st fret, followed by the middle finger on the 2nd, and the ring finger on the 3rd. Do that for every string.

For this second part of the exercise, we're going to introduce every movement we have learned so far. Therefore, you need to play the string open, then the 1st fret with your index finger, your 2nd fret with your middle finger, and the 3rd fret with your ring finger. Remember to play this sequence for all the strings.

Exercise 4 – Coordination & Strength with Four Fingers

Now that you've used three out of four fingers on your fretting hands, it is time to give that pinky of yours some fretting action. The pinky is a finger we rarely use, and therefore, can be our weakest. That being said, with these exercises you'll gain enough strength to stop the world with it.

So, in this exercise you'll play your 1st fret with your index finger, the 2nd with your middle finger, the 3rd with your ring finger, and the 4th with your pinky. Repeat this action for every string.

Are you ready to have a mighty pinky? Let's do this.

FAQ : How Do I Fight Aching Pain While Stretching?

We've all gone through that when learning; pain in your hand as you're learning your ways with the guitar isn't uncommon. This is because you should always remember that there's an intense physical effort from your fretting hand when playing the guitar. Moreover, you're not used to using the muscles you need to use for playing, so you need to develop strength in them to stretch and press without pain.

In this sense, have you ever been to the gym? If you have, you know that the first week your entire body is sore. Then, as you establish a steady workout routine, your body will respond with increased strength and stamina.

So, these are the important things to check if you feel an aching pain while playing:

» **Check your posture** – Muscles in your body are connected. Therefore, the posture of your entire body is important to achieve optimum results. In this vein, checking your posture can be a game-changer in ending the pain.

So, make sure your back is straight, your shoulders are relaxed, and your thumb sits comfortably behind the fretboard without wrapping it around it.

» **Take rests** – Sometimes, if you push them too hard, muscles get tense and sore. Therefore, the moment you start feeling pain (or even before so) you should take a rest. Don't worry, I'm not a severe teacher, we can carry on the next day!

» **Just relax** – Being anxious or nervous because your hands are sore and you can't play what your mind wants is usually a tension raiser. As tension goes up, muscles get stiff, and the results are usually worse. So, take your time for information to sink in and practice every lesson slowly, advancing little by little.

Stretching, regardless of the distance, shouldn't cause your fingers to hurt. In case you need an iconic example, you can think of Angus Young's small hands and the riff to "Back in Black". The riff requires the player to stretch the hand from fret 2 to fret 7. He can pull it off night after night with the tiniest hands. Therefore, with practice, you can play whatever you want without feeling pain.

Lastly, let's do the same but the other way around. Start with the highest notes on the thinnest string and go down fret by fret, string by string.

Conclusion

By now, you must have played the above exercises enough to have a stronger hand with increased accuracy, and an even stronger desire to learn more. If that's the case, then you're on the right path to mastering guitar playing.

In the next chapter, we'll learn our first chords and we will need those fingers more than ever. So, practice, practice, practice, and I'll see you in chapter 2 for more fun in the shape of basic chords.

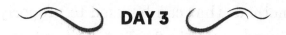

CHAPTER 2

YOUR FIRST 5 CHORDS

DAY 3

We will start with two basic sounding chord type, Major and minor. They are relatively easy to learn yet most useful for playing songs.

Buckle up, because the journey starts right now; let's do this!

But before we get to chords, you need to make sure your guitar is in tune. If you know how to tune your guitar, feel free to skip to the next subtopic. If not….

Tune Your Guitar

Guitars, just like any other stringed instrument, need to go through a process called "tuning". Tuning is a simple process where you get the strings of your guitar to sound out specific notes when you play them open. This series of notes is called "standard tuning". Standard tuning is setting up the strings to play the following open notes:

» 6th (thickest) string: E

» 5th string: A

» 4th string: D

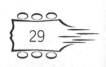

» 3rd string: G

» 2nd string: B

» 1st (thinnest) string: E

Eddie Ate Dynamite Good-Bye Eddie — a good phrase to help remember the string names.

Using an electronic tuner

There are several methods that can be used to properly tune a guitar, but at first, I'll be looking at what is (by far) the easiest and most accurate, especially for a beginner - using an electronic tuner.

All electronic tuners work essentially in the same way. They measure the sonic frequency of a note as it rings out, and there is a small display on the tuner itself that will tell you what that note is.

If your string is "out of tune", then the tuner will tell you if you are flat (lower pitch) or sharp (higher pitch). You then adjust the tuning machine to add or take away tension so that the note will be perfectly referenced to the right frequency. Most (if not all) tuners will let you know when the note is correct, either by changing colors or having some sort of indicator that flashes.

> **PRO TIP:** There are a lot of free to use tuner apps available on your phone. They're great alternatives to an electric tuner.

How to tune your guitar

Let's say that we are using an electronic tuner, for simplicity. And that our sixth string shows D# instead of E. Looking at the order of the notes, you'll notice that D# comes right before E. So, your string is tuned lower than the note it's supposed to be.

You'll need to slowly tighten the string by moving the 'tuning peg' in a counter-clockwise motion. In order to do this in a controlled manner, we play the open-string, and we start moving the tuning peg of the guitar as the string is making a sound. The electronic tuner will react to this change and show in real time the tuning of the string as you tighten it. Stop turning as soon as the display on the tuner shows that it is dead set on E (for this example). Most cases display turns green.

Usually, it is easier to approach a note from below than loosening a string to a target note. The tuning will tend to be much more stable as the tension will tend to stay consistent as it is brought up to pitch, rather than brought down.

Tuning is a necessary evil, for sure. You simply can't play properly if the notes aren't in the right relationship to each other. You'll get to the point where your ear will tell you if things just don't sound as they normally do. When that happens, you're most likely out of tune.

Chords, the Building Blocks of Modern Music

Today, you're going to learn something that you will continue to use every time you pick up your guitar your entire life.

Yes, chords are THAT important.

Undeniably, chords will be your mightiest allies to play your favorite tunes, create original music, and join friends to make musical magic. Furthermore, you'll very likely play more chords on your guitar than any other thing; even more so at the beginning.

This is because chords are the unsung heroes in the history of music. They are the building blocks upon which most Western music is built. Moreover, chords can be found in any and all music styles; going from death metal to pop and everything in between.

Yes, before you ask, electronic music is also built using chords over the beat.

But, hey, not so fast! What is a chord?

Well, a chord is a specific series of notes played at the same time. In other words, every chord is a particular blend of notes. Therefore, each chord we play, with its particular note combination, generates a certain tone that can give any song its mood, colors, and feeling.

What do I mean by mood, colors, and feeling? Well, chords convey feelings and that's why they are a great foundation to build melodies upon. These melodies built over chords are deeply related, not only to the notes of the chord, but also to the feelings these chords convey.

Am I going too fast here? Let's slow down.

Pick up your guitar. It has six strings, and these strings can give you a note each. If you strum it without your fingers on the fretboard, you'll see that you'll get six notes: E, A, D, G, B, and E.

Now, if you fret specific notes in some strings, as seen in chapter one, and combine those notes with certain finger shapes, you can create relationships between notes. These relationships are what we call chords.

Are you ready to learn chords and make a giant leap in your guitar learning career?

Well, get those fingers ready and bring your guitar, because here we go!

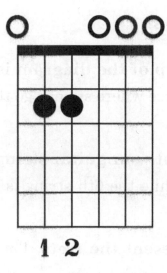

How Are Chords Named?

Before diving into how to play the chord above, it is important that you know how chords receive their names. Don't worry, it is as easy as learning the alphabet (remember... first grade?). You can use the letters of the alphabet starting from the A to the G. Therefore, your chords will be A, B, C, D, E, F, and G.

When you see only the capital letter, it is always a major chord. If you see a small "m" next to it, it means it is a minor chord.

In the case of the example, we have a capital E and a small "m". This means this chord is an E minor.

What are Chord Diagrams?

You can think of a chord diagram as a map. This map will tell you what notes to play and where to put your fingers while playing to create the intended chord.

The way they work is very simple: they are a graphic representation of your fretboard as if it was vertically oriented, looking up.

How to Read Chord Diagrams?

» **The thicker line on top of the diagram is the nut of your guitar** (the little white or black piece where strings go through before reaching the tuners).

» **Vertical lines represent your guitar strings.** The 1st string is always the furthest to the right while the 6th string is always the furthest to the left.

» **Horizontal lines represent the frets.** I'm sure you remember them from the last chapter; they are the pieces of metal dividing your fretboard.

» **Black dots represent your fingers.** Therefore, you have to place them over the string and at the fret indicated by the diagram.

» **The numbers represent the fingers you should use to play the chord.** They follow these criteria:

1 = Index finger

2 = Middle finger

3 = Ring finger

4 = Pinky or little finger

» The circles or X you'll find after the nut will mean:

» Circles signal open strings that ring without any finger on the fretboard.

» An X means that the string shouldn't ring as you play the chord (it's because they generate a note that's not part of the chord).

How to Play the Em Chord?

Let's get started by reading the chord diagram. It is important that you have your guitar handy because this is going to be 100% practical teaching.

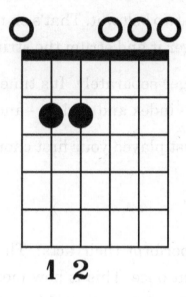

Let's follow the diagram. Hold the guitar with your fretboard facing you vertically again. Each vertical line represents a string, and each horizontal line represents a fret. If we go string by string, left to right, the leftmost is the thickest string (string 6), and the rightmost is the thinnest one (string 1).

On string 5, the second one counting from left, we see a circle with the number one below it. The thick horizontal line being zero, each line below is a fret. This spot is between the 1st and 2nd fret, but we consider this the 2nd fret. Try to locate that spot on your guitar.

There's a number one below the circle. That means we have to use finger 1 on that spot - your index finger. Fret it and play that string only - try to use only enough pressure so that the string rings without a buzz, but not more than necessary.

Now, with your left-hand index finger in place, strum all the strings at once with your right hand. It doesn't matter how it sounds - it won't sound perfect since we're still missing one finger in this chord. But give it a try anyway.

Now release the finger to give it a break. Find the position for the next finger, the circle with the number two below it. That's on the following string, again on the 2nd fret. Try to finger it and strum the strings with your right hand.

Good, we've tried each finger separately. It's time for the moment of truth. Add both fingers together - index and middle - and strum the strings.

Congratulations, you've just played your first chord!

Do You Feel Like a Juggler?

Have you seen jugglers perform their acts? They arc constantly paying attention to many things at once. This is how most of us felt when playing our first chords: paying attention to everything at the same time, nervous, making too much pressure, watching our other fingers so open strings will ring, also the hand posture, the back posture, and the buzzing sounds... it seems as too much at first.

Yet, don't worry; with practice, you'll be able to play them effortlessly time and again.

Believe me, once you master the techniques in this book, you'll be playing countless songs and chords effortlessly. Don't give up; the fun comes two seconds after effort.

The Ultimate Chord-Playing Checklist

If your Em chord doesn't sound right to your ears, worry not, because with this simple and fast checklist we'll review every step, find what's not going well, and fix it on the spot.

With your fretting hand still on the fretboard, play each string separately. What do you hear?

1. Check the pressure of your fretting hand – If you hear a note that sounds "dead" it is because you are either not pressing enough or pressing too much. To correct this, lift your finger and re-place it until it sounds good.

2. Watch for buzzing sounds – If you hear buzzing sounds this means that you're either fingering too far away from the fret, too close, or on top. To correct this move your finger within the fret limits until you find the sweet spot where it sounds good.

3. Beware of unintended string muting – When you place some fingers on the fretboard, especially at the beginning, one of the fingers you're not using for the chord might fall gracefully over another string and mute it. To correct this, look down on your fretting hand and make sure your other fingers are away from the strings.

This is a checklist that works for any chord and that you should use every time you have problems with a particular chord. Again, don't get frustrated, just find the issue, correct it, and move on. You'll be playing your favorite songs in no time.

PRO TIP: Take Frequent Breaks Until You Build Muscle

Imagine walking into a gym for the first time and trying to do Chris Hemsworth, Serena Williams, Dwayne Johnson, or Cristiano Ronaldo's workout routine the first day; impossible, right?

Well, your hand muscles aren't too different from your pectorals or biceps; you need to build their strength by playing. So, if it hurts, don't push it too much, just take a break and come back with refreshed energy.

At first, hand positions could seem bizarre, but with a bit of practice, you'll get used to them, and they'll feel natural and comfortable.

Don't worry if it takes you long to put all the fingers in place! It takes plenty of time at first to finger a chord.

Moving On; More Chords!

Let's add some more important chords to your library of resources. With each chord you learn and play properly, you'll be one step closer to playing your favorite tunes and having the time of your life playing the guitar.

The E Chord

You've seen Em or E minor. Let's take a look at its major version. As we said above, when chords are major, we just use the capital letter. So, this is your E chord.

E chord is simple but it's important that you get the sound right. You can refer to the audio track in bonus section and verify if you're playing the chord correctly.

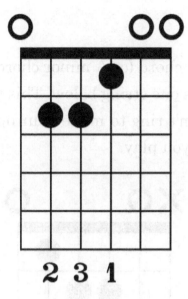

To build this chord up, you need to add one more finger to the previous shape to turn the minor chord into a major chord. The note you need to add is at the first fret on the 3rd string. We're going to change the fingers a bit; your index finger goes to the 3rd string while the middle and ring fingers occupy the 5th and 4th string respectively.

Remember, if it doesn't sound great, just go back to the checklist and find out where the problem is. Fix it and try again. Practice, practice, practice, and it will all feel effortless shortly, I promise.

PRO TIP: Can You Feel the Difference?

Major chords sound fuller and happier than minor chords which sound a tad darker and sadder. Can you feel that difference when playing these chords? That's exactly what we meant at the beginning: chords convey emotions.

The Am Chord

We could say that the Am chord (or A minor chord) is very similar in shape to the E chord but it starts one string below. This time, we have to mind our 6th string since it shouldn't ring to make your open 5th sting (which is A, btw) be the lowest sound you play.

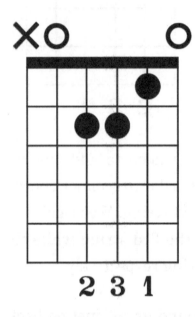

PRO TIP: When learning this chord is very common to touch, unintentionally, the bottom string with your index finger as you're fretting the second string on the first fret. Use the checklist above to correct this but don't despair, you'll get to make it sound perfect shortly.

The A Chord

As we saw before, removing the little "m" from the title gives us a major chord, so this is the A major chord.

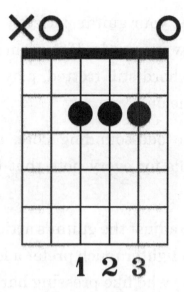

To play this chord correctly, you have to put three fingers vertically one above the other on the second fret. As you've seen in the diagram, you'll use your index finger for the 4th string, the middle finger for the 3rd string, and the ring finger on your 2nd string.

Although it might feel a little awkward and you might think that your fingers are overcrowded too tightly into one spot. Fear not, I've seen players like Kingfisher play an A chord that way (or other, much more precise and complicated things) with their massive fingers effortlessly.

Practice and it will feel natural very soon; I promise.

FAQ : How Much Pressure is Enough Pressure?

This is a big issue, especially for beginners. How do you know how much pressure is enough pressure? Well, there is a thin red line between pressing enough and pressing too much. But again, how do you know you're pressing too much? Well, excessive pressure will cause the note to be out of tune. Indeed, the more you press, the more you'll increase the note's pitch.

Therefore, to test this, tune your guitar perfectly and then fret, let's say A major chord, and hear how it sounds. If it seems odd or out of tune, grab your tuner and, with the chord still fretted, play one note at a time to see which one is the out-of-tune one.

Once you've identified the odd-sounding note, try pressing less until it sounds in tune. Repeat this for every note that the tuner tells you is not on-pitch.

With time, you can learn to adjust the guitar's action to match your pressure. In this vein, players with a lighter touch prefer a lower action (strings closer to the fretboard), and those who like pressing harder prefer a higher string action (more space between the string and the fretboard).

The D Chord

This is the final chord we'll see today, so bear with me just for a little longer. Plus, the D chord is among my favorites; it's got a sweet and happy sound that just makes me smile; I hope the same thing happens to you.

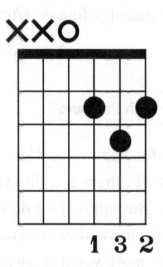

PRO TIP: To avoid confusing major and minor chords, just use your ear to distinguish a sad or dark-sounding chord from an uplifting, happy-sounding one. If it feels like the first; it's minor. If it feels like the second, it's major.

To play the D chord correctly, you need to play only the four bottom strings. This is good practice for your picking hand's accuracy. Furthermore, the way you need to place your fingers to form a chord might feel a little awkward at the beginning with the middle finger on the 1st string, the ring finger on the 2nd, and the ring finger on the 3rd. Don't worry, with practice, you'll land on it perfectly and enjoy its beautiful sound for years to come.

DAY 4

No new chords today! You can revise what you learnt in day 3 or simply take a day off.

Memorize all the shapes and get your fingers comfortable with them before diving in tomorrow.

See you tomorrow!

CHAPTER 3

LEARNING CHORD SHIFTS

DAY 5

What Are Chord Progressions?

Just as a combination of notes is a chord, a combination of chords is a chord progression. This means that to create a chord progression, you have to play one chord after the other forming a sequence.

The key to understanding chord progressions is talking about intervals rather than notes. Although there are a limitless number of possible chord progressions, most modern music is based only on a few of them.

So, the good news is that by learning only a handful of chords (well, maybe, two handfuls of chords) you'll be able to play a huge number of songs. Furthermore, knowing these chord progressions can even open the door for you to create your original tunes as well.

The Secrets to Successful Chord Switching

You've been learning how to play certain chords and going through a checklist to make each of them sound great. Well, it is time for us to take this a little further and practice how to go from one chord to another. This will allow you to follow a chord progression and play your first song.

I know, you must be thinking: "but playing one chord correctly takes me ages, how can I play two in a row and fast?!" Well, worry not, because this book is like an information highway straight to the heart of guitar playing.

So, buckle up because in the next 3 days we'll go through all the most common chords and you'll learn the secret pros use around the world to make fast and effortless chord changes: transitioning using the smallest finger movements possible.

Oh, and don't worry if you don't remember every chord by heart yet; with time and practice, you definitely will.

Moving from Am to E

This is a great example of how, when we use our fingers like a single block, we can move from one chord to another effortlessly.

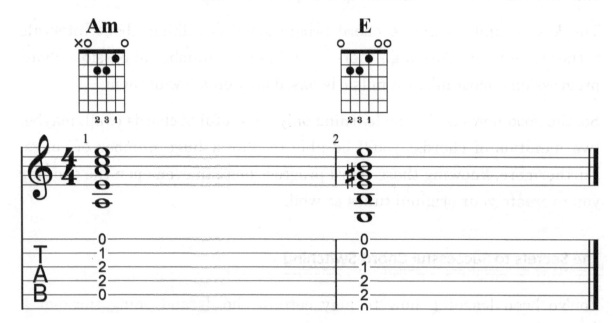

As you might remember, Am and E share the same exact shape with the difference that the Am chord is played one string below the E chord.

So, for this exercise simply loosen your fingers enough to make it possible to move them from one chord to the next, and then slowly move your hand up. Once you're in the E-chord position, press the strings again to make the chord sound good.

Practice doing this a few times until you feel comfortable going from the Am chord to the E chord and back. If your hand feels tired or you feel any pain, stop, take a break, and carry on with fresh, relaxed muscles.

> **PRO TIP:** When moving your hand as a block, bear in mind that you shouldn't lift your fingers from the strings; on the opposite, you should loosen them just enough to make the change.

Moving from A to Em

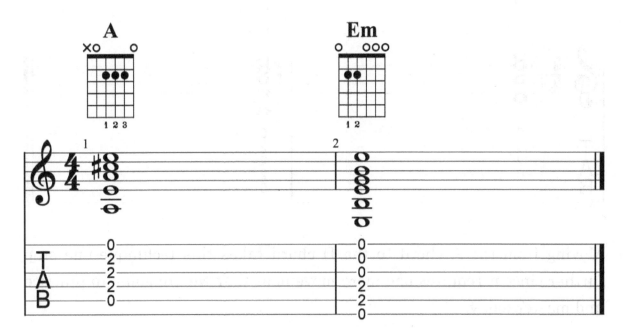

I'm sure you remember your first chord ever played: the Em chord. Also, by now, you should be familiar with the A chord as well. Well, changing from one to another requires only two movements that can be done almost as a block.

What you should do is move your entire hand up one string and lift your ring finger since it's not part of the Em chord. So, as you did before, loosen the index and middle fingers and move them up one string while lifting the ring finger enough to avoid touching your third string, which should ring freely.

Practice this movement back and forth a few times until you feel the change is comfortable.

Moving from D to A

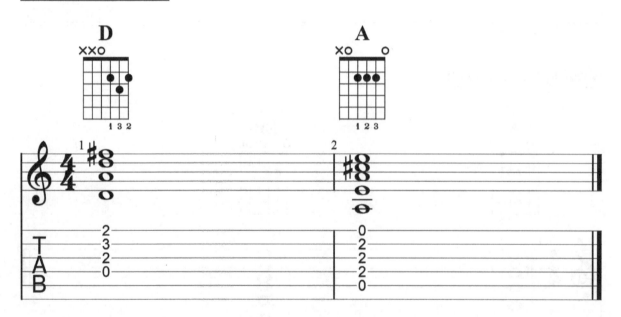

Moving from the A chord to the D chord takes this technique one step further since it requires one more movement that we are going to practice and master today.

Remember that the D chord requires our index and middle fingers to be in the same line at the 2nd fret. This is while our ring finger occupies the 2nd string at the 3rd fret.

So, what you will learn how to do is move your index and middle fingers up while you move your ring finger horizontally from the 3rd fret to the second fret. With time, you will do this effortlessly in one movement, but for now, we'll practice the following sequence:

1. Loosen and move your index and middle fingers one string up.

2. Loosen and move your ring finger to the 2nd fret keeping it at the same string.

3. Strum the chord.

Follow this scheme to go from D to A and do the opposite to go from A to D; first, move your ring finger horizontally and then, your index and middle fingers vertically.

Day 5 is a wrap! Well done, you've mastered three chord changes! That deserves a celebration, but not too much because we have a lot to learn on day 6.

 **DAY 6**

Mastering Three-Chord Changes

Welcome to day 6, I hope you're rested and motivated because today is not just another day; it is a pivotal moment in your life as a musician. Why you might wonder. Well, because today you'll learn how to make three-and-four-chord changes which means you can play your first song.

For example, I imagine you are familiar with the song "Sweet Home Alabama". Well, the entire song uses three chords, so after today you can start playing some tunes and having even more fun.

Are you ready to apply everything you've learned so far in two exercises?

Let's do this!

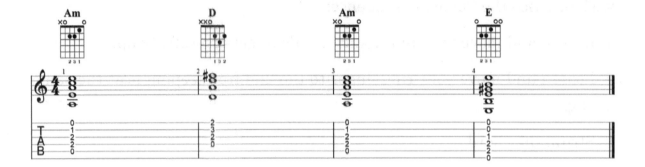

Congratulations, with this first exercise, you can already play your first song. That being said, let's do another one.

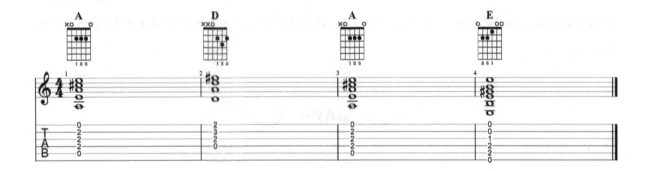

For the above exercise, I'd encourage you to listen to audio track and internalize the sound and try to follow along. You can get the audio track in the bonus section

> **PRO TIP:** These exercises are about precision and getting familiar with the movements, not about speed. Therefore, focus on making every chord sound good rather than on making quick changes. Believe me, once your muscle memory kicks in, you'll be doing effortless changes in no time. But for now "slow and accurate" is the name of the game.
>
> Furthermore, you can use the checklist to make every chord sound perfect.
>
> That's a wrap again! Go get some rest because day 7 is full of fun lessons and a lot of guitar playing.

FAQ : How to Practice Chord Shifting?

Chord shifting is one of the core abilities guitar players need to master. Moreover, it is one that we continue to get better at throughout all our playing life. Therefore, learning how to do it correctly from day one can prove to be a game-changer.

Let's see two fabulous tips for that:

» **Learn one chord at a time** – Before you try changing from one chord to the next, make sure you have both shapes memorized. This is because if you're doubtful about where your fingers should go, you'll waste time between chords. Therefore, make sure you know them both thoroughly and play them separately before attempting the shift.

» **Start from the lowest note** – Think of your fingers forming the chord as if they were "cascading" down from the lowest note to the highest note. With this method, you can form the chord worrying about the position of one finger at a time. This is a more efficient approach than trying to land all notes at the same time.

DAY 7

A Longer Chord Progression

I know, you probably read the title and went bananas thinking this is going to be really hard. Well, don't worry because it is the exact opposite; we'll be working on the same skills we worked on yesterday and using the same techniques to get even more results.

That being said, today you'll be introduced to a guitar playing style that has been one of the most important in guitar history: blues music. Indeed, today you'll learn a typical blues chord progression that can be found in an infinite number of songs and will help you jam with other musicians as well.

So, if you have a friend who's a seasoned player and likes soloing over a blues base, you can practice these exercises a lot and then ask him or her to join you and play a solo over your chords.

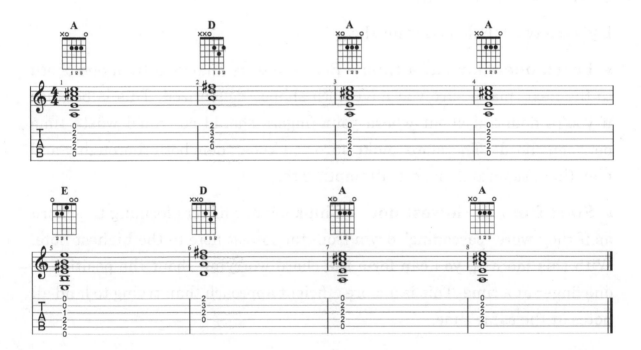

Conclusion

Congratulations! You've made it to the end of the chord changes lesson and you're ready to play your first songs. Indeed, learning to change chords opens the doors to playing countless songs.

Moreover, what you've learned in this lesson will accompany you for the time you play guitar since it is the foundation of most Western music.

Although you might be thinking "yeah, but it takes ages to change from one chord to the next" and you're probably right, time and practice will work their magic and allow you to master these techniques in no time.

So, practice, practice, practice, and take breaks. Don't get frustrated, playing music with friends is just around the corner.

☰ CHAPTER 4 ☰

YOUR PICKING HAND ALSO MATTERS

 DAY 8

Strumming? What's that?

Music is built using three aspects: harmony, melody, and rhythm. With notes we can build a melody, with chords we can create harmony, and our picking hand will give it the rhythm.

So, in this chapter, you'll learn how to strum your guitar to create a rhythm pattern that can help the harmony created by the chord progression. But, what does it mean to "strum" my guitar? Well, strumming is a movement made with your picking hand to pick various strings with a single stroke using sweeping movements.

These sweeping movements are the ones that create the rhythm pattern. Mastering the picking hand and rhythm is the secret of guitar legends like Keith Richards, Malcolm Young, Nile Rodgers, Pete Townshend, and James Hetfield among many, many others.

Therefore, while your fretting hand is busy going from chord to chord, your right hand will also be busy following a rhythm pattern. This pattern is what makes people dance, clap, sing, and move their hands and heads to the music.

Finally, the picking hand is also what makes the guitar the quintessential instrument to accompany a singer (or your own voice). The guitar is capable of producing all three elements needed to make music happen.

Are you ready to make people dance, clap, and cheer?

Let's get started!

Starting Out with Muted Notes

We want to focus all your attention on the picking hand. Therefore, we will strum what we call "dead strings" and focus solely on following the rhythm pattern. But, how do you mute the strings? Well, you just have to place your fretting hand over the strings touching them without applying any pressure.

This way, strings will sound "muffled" or "dead" and you can focus 100% of your attention on your picking hand. You'll see that the muted note is represented in the tab with an x where the fret number should be.

Using muted notes makes it easier to focus on practicing your strumming for now without having to worry about what chords you finger with your left hand.

Upstrokes & Downstrokes

Strumming is a movement that helps you pick all strings with a single pick swing. This swing goes down but also goes up (unless you're trying to sound like Johnny Ramone, right?).

Usually, strumming patterns include both movements. This means that you'll play the strings when your hand goes down and also pick them when it goes back up. The first movement is known as a downstroke while the second is known as an upstroke.

Up until now, you have been using mostly downward strokes but now we are going to be more efficient and use your upward movements as well. For this, you can think of your picking arm as creating an imaginary circle that happens to touch the strings between the bridge and the neck.

> **PRO TIP:** Pick thickness does matter and you'll see it makes a big difference in this case. If, when moving upward, your pick gets stuck between the strings, you're either holding it too tightly or the pick is too stiff. Try a lighter gauge, around 0.50 millimeters. These picks are more fragile but their tip folds when it touches the strings making the movement easier.

In tabs, a downward stroke is represented with this symbol:

And an upward stroke with this one:

> While doing open strumming, make sure you are plucking all the strings. You can check out the audio track available in the bonus section for reference.

Learning Your First Strumming Patterns

Now that we are clear about how to properly practice strumming patterns, it is time to practice some of the most common ones. Just like it happened with chords, most strumming patterns in popular songs repeat making it easy to play a great number of songs utilizing just a handful of them.

We'll be using, at least for now, the string-deadening technique you just learned.

Dividing Time; Let's Talk Time Signatures

Time and tempo are paramount to playing tablatures correctly. But, how do we read a time signature? Well, it is very simple.

The time signature is divided into two numbers: one at the bottom and one at the top.

The top number tells you how many beats each time signature has. The bottom number will tell you the value of those beats.

So, for example, if your tablature reads 4/4, it means that one bar has four beats and that each beat is a quarter note (it is divided by 4). Another example could be the 3/4 time signature in which the bar is still divided in quarter notes, but you play 3 beats per bar.

Quarter Notes Rhythm

So, to begin with, rhythm-wise, we'll use quarter notes. What are quarter notes? Well, remember what we just learned; they occupy one beat each. So, if your bar has four beats, you'll play them four times per bar.

In other words, every strum is a beat.

If you're thinking, even for a minute, that you can't follow a rhythm, don't worry. Again, you're in the right place to learn everything from scratch to proficiency. Moreover, if you can count to four (1, 2, 3, 4... just like in first grade) you can practice, and, with time and practice, create a perfect rhythm with your right hand (watch out Keith!).

Furthermore, we went the extra mile for you and made an audio example of how it should sound so you can follow and practice. Go to our audio samples and listen, then repeat.

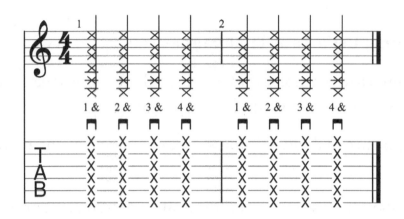

Eighth Notes Rhythm

To count eighth notes in four-beat bars, we need to divide every beat into two strokes or strums. This would be like counting 1, & 2, & 3, & 4, & 1… In other words, you'll play twice the number of strums in the same time frame you just played 4 in the last exercise. Yes, what you're thinking is correct; this means playing twice as fast (look out Johnny!).

There is also an audio clip for this so you can hear the example and how it should sound.

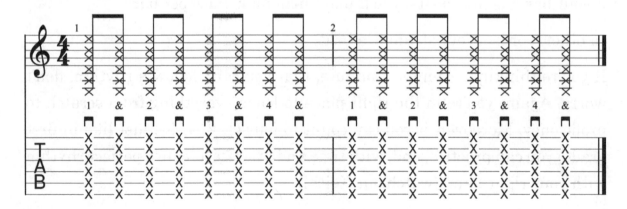

Next, do the same but with an upstroke on every second note. Every number should be a downstroke, and every "&" an upstroke. With some practice, this creates a steady up-and-down flow with your right hand. Listen to the audio to see how it should sound.

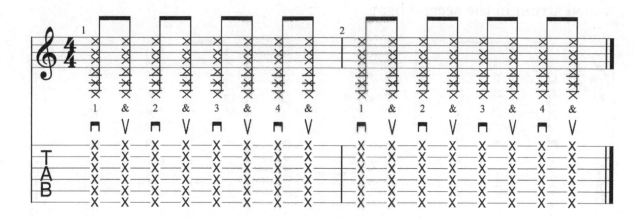

PRO TIP: This is something that really helped me when I was learning the same thing you're learning now. Sit on a chair next to a table or desk and, using your index finger, hit the table with every beat. If you do this for some time, you'll realize you're hitting the table in every beat and reaching the highest point with your finger exactly between beats.

The moment your finger hits the table you're marking quarter notes. When your finger is up in the opposite position, you're marking an eight note. Add to this saying the "1 & 2 &…" out loud utilizing the number when hitting the table and the "&" when in the air. This is an exercise for your picking hand.

Quarter & Eighth Note Combination Rhythm

Now that you've mastered quarter and eighth notes on their own, it's time to combine them. For the first exercise, you should use the following rhythm pattern: 1, 2 & 3, 4. This will sound close to the first exercise but with an added strum in the second beat.

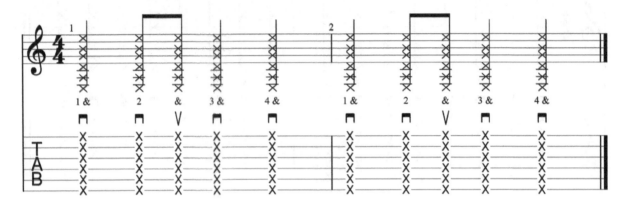

For the second exercise, we'll add another strum for the fourth beat. Therefore, your new rhythm pattern formula reads like this: 1, 2 & 3, 4 &.

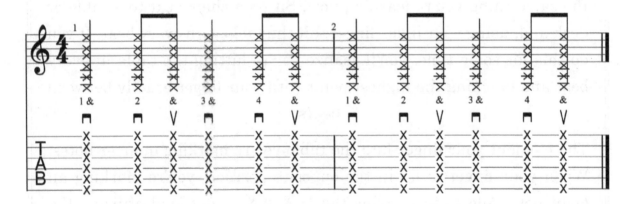

I think this is enough information for 24 hours, so let's leave it here and call it a day.

Let your picking hand rest and we'll meet tomorrow to add chords to these patterns so we are one step closer to playing your favorite songs.

FAQ : How Do I Improve My Left-Hand, Right-Hand Sync?

Your fretting hand needs to be performing one duty while your picking hand is performing another. This is a fact all guitar players know about and have to embrace to be able to play successfully. Therefore, practicing the sync between your left and right hand is paramount to guitar playing at every stage of the path.

But how do I practice improving this synchronization? Well, let me give you two pieces of valuable advice I wish I was given when starting out:

» **Don't strum until the chord is right** – A very common mistake all of us made, especially when starting out, is to strum with the picking hand before the fretting hand is ready. As a result, our chord will sound tortuous and odd. To prevent this from happening, always make sure the fretting hand is ready, you've memorized the chord, and you've played them successfully on their own before making the shift. Remember, playing slow and accurate first is paramount to play it fast and accurate shortly.

» **Pick the notes you pick** – Every guitar player in the world knows that tempo is king, but building accuracy is a must as well. Therefore, you can't overlook either of your hands when playing and chord shifting. So, if you're plucking different strings than you're fretting, stop immediately and slow the process. Go back to playing each chord separately, and finally, attempt to play it at half speed keeping your eyes on your picking hand. Once you've mastered it, you can speed up as much as you like.

DAY 9

Strumming Chords

We've been getting ready for this moment; it's time for the real deal! Yes, we're going to use the strumming patterns we saw yesterday but this time we'll play them with real chords. Don't worry; we'll play chords and patterns you already know, so all you need to do is apply what you've been practicing until now.

Today, both your hands will see a lot of action. Are you ready to be one step closer to playing countless songs on your guitar?

Here we go!

Strumming Patterns on One Chord

We'll start with the first chord you learned how to play and the first rhythm you played. This means you should place your fingers in the Em chord position and play downstrokes on every beat. So, counting 1, 2, 3, 4, you'll have to make the Em chord sound good following the beat.

> **PRO TIP:** Counting out loud can be a great help for this exercise. Indeed, saying the numbers out loud as you're lowering your hand for every stroke will help you stay on the beat, nailing the rhythm. With time, the counting will become only mental.

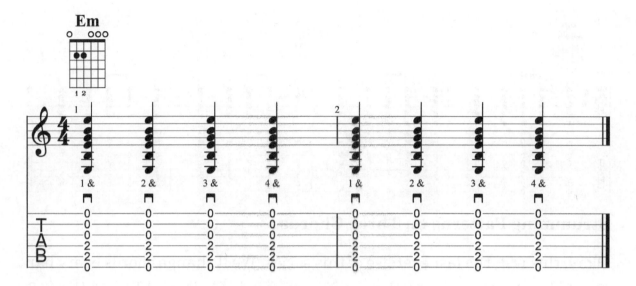

Strumming Patterns on Two Chords

Once you've managed to get the previous exercise sounding good, let's try to change chords every two bars. Don't worry if you miss a beat changing from one chord to another; it is completely normal. With time and practice, I promise your chord changes will be smooth as silk and you'll never miss a beat because of them.

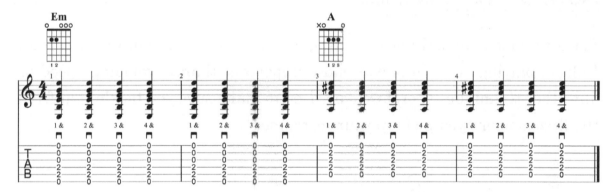

Now, for this second exercise, let's spice it up a little and follow the 1, 2 &, 3, 4 rhythm pattern with the same chords changing them every two bars. Again, if you miss a beat trying to change the chord, don't worry; with practice, you'll nail every change in the correct beat.

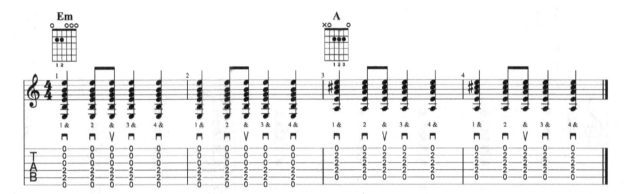

Strumming Patterns on Three Chords

Okay, this is it, the last exercise of this series. We'll change chords every bar (every four beats) utilizing three different chords (A, D, and E) and the 1, 2 & 3, 4 rhythm pattern. This is an exercise that takes time to master, but it represents a giant leap in your guitar mastery path.

Just like Neil Armstrong said: "a small chord change exercise, a giant leap for that man's guitar playing skills."

FAQ : How do I Keep My Tempo?

Perfect tempo is something all of us, guitar players, chase our entire career. Indeed, playing on time is way more important than developing speed or any other technique. Therefore, you need to make sure you tackle that from the first moment you pick up your instrument.

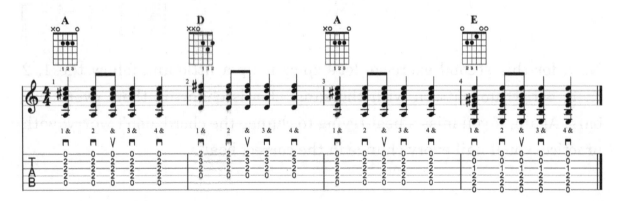

But, how do you practice to improve your tempo? The answer is very simple: never practice without a metronome. By this I mean every time you pick up your guitar to practice is another chance to get better with your tempo; so make sure you don't miss it and use a metronome.

Finally, you have a million options between analog, digital, and apps. So, there's no excuse not to use one. Furthermore, you might feel you're going ahead of the beat or behind the beat; don't worry, it's normal.

The more you practice with a metronome, the better you'll get at it.

Conclusion

Congratulations! You've made it through the basics; you've laid the foundations for a successful playing career with your guitar. Moreover, you've done so over solid ground with the building blocks that will make your guitar-playing empire solid and lasting.

Perhaps, at this point, you still feel a little like a juggler taking care of everything at once. Don't worry about it; you're taking huge steps in the right direction. Moreover, with enough practice, you'll be playing songs in less than a week from now.

Speaking of which, we'll add some more chords to your library in the following chapter so you can extend your vocabulary and play even more songs.

Go rest your hands and recharge your batteries; I'll see you in the next chapter with obnoxious amounts of fun and a ton of info.

CHAPTER 5

CHORDS, CHORDS, AND MORE CHORDS!

DAY 10

More Chords!

There are countless possible chords in every guitar. Indeed, our instrument is very close to being an infinite canvas to create the most beautiful sonic landscapes. Because of this, the road to learning chords is never-ending; you can always add more to your library. This will always make your playing more colorful, interesting, and appealing.

In the past 9 days, you've mastered some chords, some chord changes, and some rhythm patterns. From this moment on, we'll work on expanding those.

As we said at the beginning, we're building that path with solid stones, little by little. Therefore, in this book, we'll cover the basics that will work as a golden ticket to playing hundreds of thousands of songs.

That is our promise, that after mastering the teachings in this book, you'll be able to play, have fun, join friends, and create your own music. Then, if the path feels comfortable, you can continue to expand your knowledge into the territories of jazz and other more complex styles of music.

In other words, the guitar is an infinite instrument with incalculable sonic possibilities that can accompany your entire life. We, guitar players, never stop learning.

So, are you ready to expand your knowledge and your chord library?

Go get your guitar, because we're going to play a lot!

The C Chord

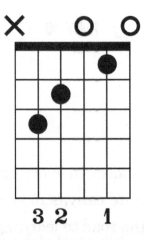

C chord shape is a bit tricky; you can check the audio track in the bonus section and to check if you're playing it right.

To play the C chord, we need to place the ring finger on string 5, the middle finger on string 4, and the index finger on string 2. Pay attention to this last one - it has to be perpendicular enough to the strings so that you don't accidentally mute string 1. Pluck every string separately to make sure they all ring well without buzzing.

The C chord uses 5 strings, so try not to strum string 6. It will still sound ok if you do, but it's better to get used to not strum it.

The G Chord

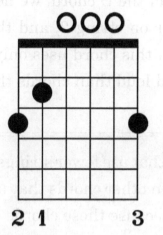

To play the G chord, we need to place the middle finger on string 6, the index finger on string 5, and the ring finger (or pinky if it's more comfortable) on string 1.

Some guitar players play this chord using the pinky and also adding the ring finger on string 2, like this:

Both ways are equally good and sound very similar, so choosing one or the other comes down to personal taste. Try them both, choose the one that's the most comfortable for you, and play it that way whenever you find a G chord.

The Dm Chord

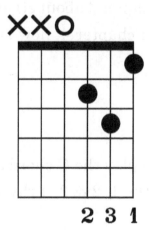

To play the minor version of the D chord, we need to use the middle finger on string 3, the ring finger on string 2, and the index finger on string 1. Like its major counterpart, this chord uses only 4 strings. Because of this, it sounds less powerful and loud than chords that use more strings, like G or Em.

> **PRO TIP:** Some chords that use fewer strings, like D, can sound a little less full or "smaller" than other chords that utilize all the strings, like G for example. This is because these chords don't need the upper two strings (A and E) and have less low-end or bass to their sound. Worry not, in the right context, they can sound less full but just as beautiful.

That's a wrap for day 10.

You have three chords to practice, practice, and practice some more. We'll meet tomorrow to add some rhythm to them and have even more fun.

DAY 11

We've learned three new chords and we're going to make them dance using some rhythm patterns. Indeed, we're going to mix this brand-new information with the one we learned in chapter 4 about strumming patterns. If you don't remember what happened in chapter 4, now is the perfect time to go look; I'll wait right here.

Exercise 1

For exercise one, you need to play the C chord and also the G chord we just learned. We'll do this using the 1, 2 & 3, 4 rhythm pattern.

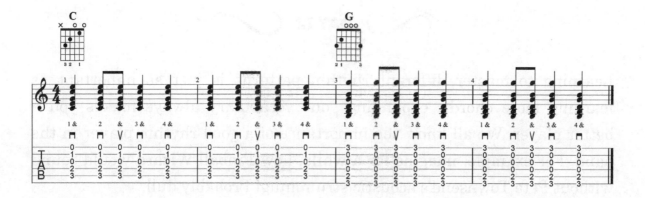

Exercise 2

For exercise 2, we shall repeat the same rhythm pattern, but let's change the chords around a bit to have more fun. We'll go from the Dm chord to the G chord, and end it with two bars of the C chord.

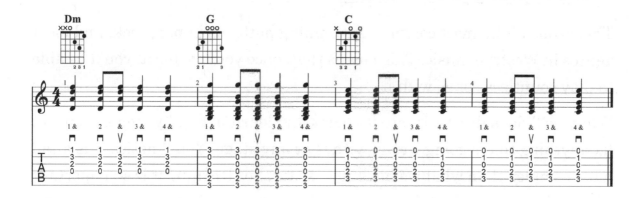

Getting used to new chord shapes and memorizing them takes time, patience, and practice. That being said, you're probably noting at this point that it takes less effort than the first time you did it in chapter 3. Well, this means you're making progress and building muscle memory and strength. So, to overcome the moment of doubt when you see a chord name and need to remember its shape, you can use a reminder by having each chord diagram close while practicing.

DAY 12

Learning to master different rhythm patterns is just as important as learning more chords; expanding your vocabulary always makes you a better player. We all know the importance of a good rhythm player in the band. For example, imagine for a while, how Pinball Wizard would sound without Pete Townsend's acoustic strumming! Probably dull.

Let's spend a day with different strumming patterns to enhance our rhythmic vocabulary

Groove is the boss!

The Omnipresent Strumming Pattern

This is one of the most common strumming patterns in pop, rock, and most genres in Western music. This means that, once you master it, you'll be able to play countless songs with it.

What we'll do is dissect it into its parts and learn it step by step so you can fix anything that's going wrong with it at any stage. You'll notice it is a tad more complex than what we have seen so far, but learning it is so important it's worth every minute of the time you spend practicing it.

To learn it properly, we'll go back to the muted strings technique and focus only on our picking hand.

Let's begin; it is a 4-beat-per-bar rhythm, so you'll have to play 1, 2, and 4 with downstrokes. Yes, you've read that correctly, it isn't a printing mistake or a writing mistake; it means that you'll be skipping the third beat. You might have noticed the "ties" connecting the 2nd and 3rd beat; these mean you're not playing the 3rd beat.

Now that you have that, let's move on and add an upstroke (&) after the second beat. You've done something very similar before, it will be something like 1, 2 & 4.

We've added an audio recording of how it should sound so make sure you hear it and copy what happens there.

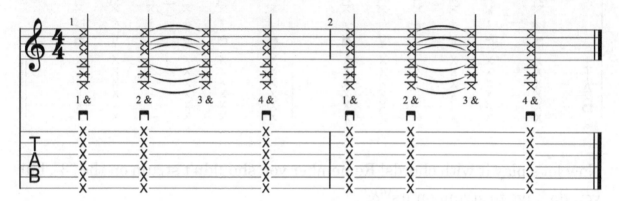

Next, add an upstroke on the "&" following the 2. Listen to the audio recordings to make sure you follow. Like this:

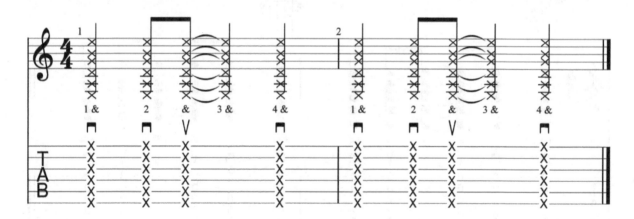

We're almost there. Now add another upstroke in the "&" after the 3. Remember that there's no stroke in the 3! There's an empty space there, which makes this strumming pattern tricky. Use that empty moment to bring your strumming hand down (without strumming) so that you're ready for another upstroke.

With this, you'll be playing the entire pattern; listen to the recording and play along to ensure you get it right.

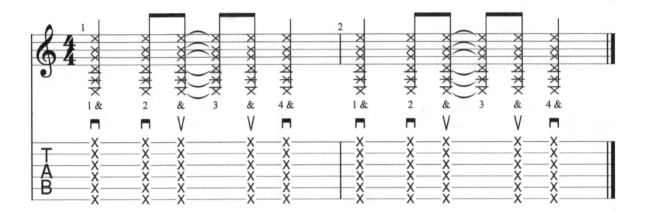

Now let's play it with chords! Remember you shouldn't strum on the "3", but you do have to strum on its "&".

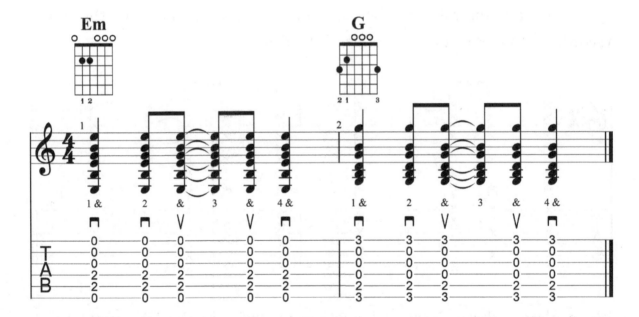

Now try this one:

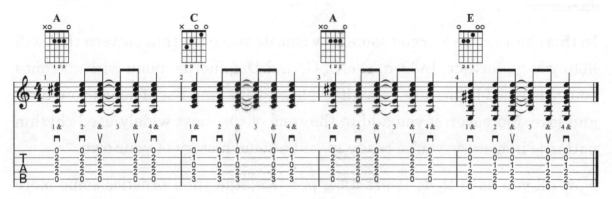

FAQ : How Long Until I Learn all the chords?

If the above statement includes the word all, then the answer is, most definitely, a lifetime.

That being said, let's focus on the statement itself. Is it important to know all the chords? Moreover, does it make a difference if you learn the chords within one week or one month? Guitar learning is not an exact science and every guitar player is different from the rest. Therefore, comparing yourself to others or to a timeframe someone gave you is a recipe for disaster.

Instead of thinking about how long will it take, I think it is more positive to think about being able to fret chords as they are named and also being fluent when shifting chords. Believe me, time and practice will turn you into a better player; no doubt about it.

Just have patience with your own hands and mind and slowly build your skills. Before you know it, you'll be playing whatever you want on the guitar.

Remember, going step by step, slowly but firmly, and building with solid foundations is more important than how long it takes. Slow and steady wins the race, ten times out of ten.

Conclusion

In this chapter, we learned some new chords and a rhythm pattern that will help you go further. Indeed, the C, G, and Dm chords along with the ones you've learned before are enough to play a very long list of songs you know and love. Moreover, if you add to that one of the most widely used rhythm patterns in history; you're ready to make some history of your own.

Now all you have to do is practice, practice, and then practice some more so you're ready to enjoy all that's coming in the next chapter. I have a little surprise for you. No, I can't tell you yet or I'll spoil it; all I can say is that you'll enjoy it a lot.

So, get some rest and be ready for tomorrow; it's going to be a super-fun day with lots of guitar playing.

≣ CHAPTER 6 ≣

POPULAR CHORD PROGRESSIONS IN MY FAVORITE SONGS

The following songs will work as a musical summary of everything you've learned so far in this book.

Moreover, this represents the target we've been pursuing from day 1: playing your favorite songs on guitar. So, these are real-life examples of how huge artists use the same resources you just learned to make arenas scream, shout, and dance.

Also, I will introduce you to a very good friend of mine that shall accompany you for as long as you play. His name is Mr. Metronome and he is the one and only tempo king. It is paramount that you practice all that's coming next with him; he will help you avoid developing bad habits and will definitely make you a better player.

In case you're wondering, the metronome isn't only my friend; he is the legends' best friend as well. Furthermore, it is very rare to find a record or album today that wasn't recorded using a metronome for every instrument.

The way it works is very simple; it is set to a fixed bpm (beats per minute). Therefore, you'll hear a distinct sound every time the 1st beat comes along and then three times the same sound for beats 2, 3, and 4.

Oh, and don't worry, you don't have to buy anything, there are a million free metronome apps and most dedicated websites offer it for free too.

You'll see a number in the following exercises, that's your bpm. It is paramount that you learn all that's coming up next using the metronome so your natural tempo improves. Moreover, by the time you finish this book, you'll very likely be so familiar with the metronome that it will be hard to play without it.

Are you ready for two days of songs, fun, more songs, and more fun?

Go get your guitar because here we go!

> **PRO TIP:** To start using the metronome, take the number I wrote in every tab and divide it by two. This will give you half the real speed. Do this even if it feels ridiculously slow and try to play every exercise without mistakes from beginning to end. Then, increase the speed little by little until you make it to normal speed. Take your time and aim for "correct" instead of "fast".

With How Many Chords Can I Start Playing Songs?

You can find songs with as little as two chords that repeat throughout them. For example, if you're a reggae fan and love Bob Marley, you can play "Lively Up" with only two chords: the D and the G chords. Also, a timeless classic like "Sweet Home Alabama" takes only three chords to play: C, G, and D.

That being said, your chord vocabulary allows you to play more songs and have more fun. Furthermore, you can also write your tunes using all the tools in your toolbox. In this vein, the more tools you can use, the more musical ground you can cover, and the better guitar player you'll be.

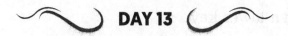

DAY 13

Some of My Favorite Chord Progressions

Em – C – G – D

I'm sure you know the smash megahit by The Cranberries called "Zombie". If you don't, it's a great moment to discover a very powerful, meaningful, and cool song that rocked the world when it came out in 1994.

> **PRO TIP:** You'll find down and up strokes in the tab's rhythm pattern but it's up to you if you want to play it entirely with downstrokes. That being said, it usually sounds a little more aggressive and is a little more demanding energy-wise to use only downward strokes rather than down-and-up strokes.

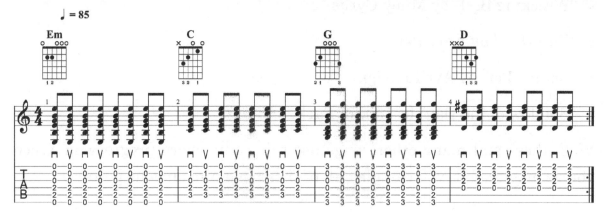

G – D – Am – G – D – C

I'm sure that you know who Bob Dylan is. Well, he is the original composer of the song "Knockin' on Heaven's Doors" which was later covered by Guns n' Roses and many other bands. This is the same chord progression he used in the original recording. It won't match the Guns n' Roses version, though, since they play it in a lower key.

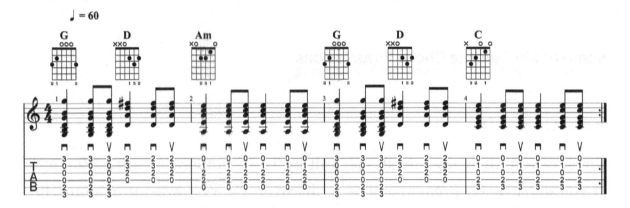

Make learning this progression more fun by playing the audio track in bonus section and following along.

G - D - Em – C

Do you recognize any of the songs on this list?

» "Don't Stop Believing" by Journey

» "Wrecking Ball" by Miley Cyrus

» "Firework" by Katy Perry

» "Sk8ter Boi" by Avril Lavigne

» "Shadow of the Day" by Linkin Park

Well, these and many other songs use this same chord progression. Once you've mastered it, you can play all of these five hits on your guitar.

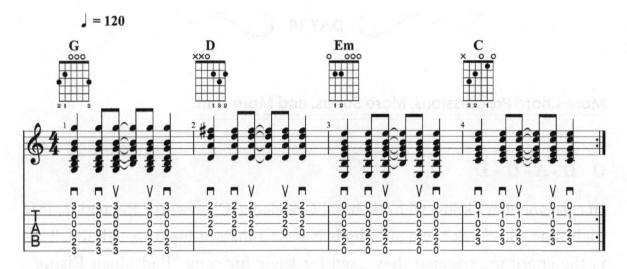

Am - G – C

Vance Joy is an amazing Australian songwriter that took the world by storm with his hit #1 single "Riptide". This is the chord progression Vance used to turn the world in his direction with that song. You'll see the tempo is quite higher, remember to work your way there slowly.

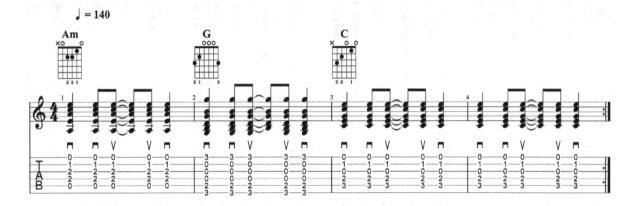

All right! That's a wrap for day 13, I hope you liked my surprise and had fun playing some of the core chord progressions used by my idols (that hopefully become yours too).

Get some rest because we have more songs and a ton of fun coming up tomorrow!

DAY 14

More Chord Progressions, More Songs, and More Fun!

G - D - A - G – D

In case you don't know who the band Creedence Clearwater Revival is, it is high time you check them out and become an instant fan as we all did. This is the chord progression they used for their hit song "Bad Moon Rising". Chances are you'll fall in love with John Fogerty's voice forever.

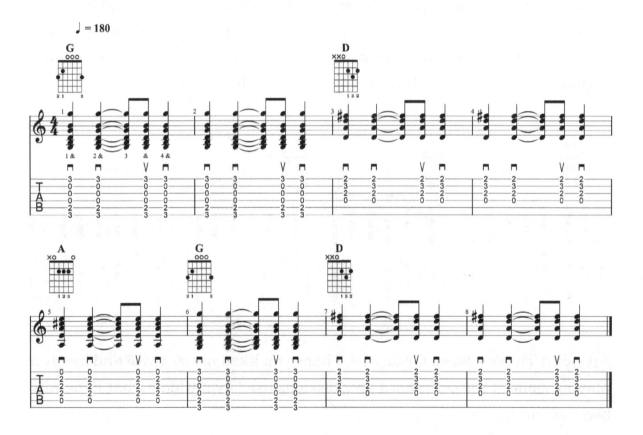

D - A - D - G - D - A – D

Perhaps, you heard about an English band that was quite famous in the sixties called The Beatles. Well, their hit song "Hey Jude" (if you've never heard it, please do so) was built around this chord progression.

Although the chord progression is the same, they play it in a higher pitch. You can play it at the same tone they do if you put a capo on your guitar's third fret. If you've never used one, don't worry, we'll talk about capos later on in this book.

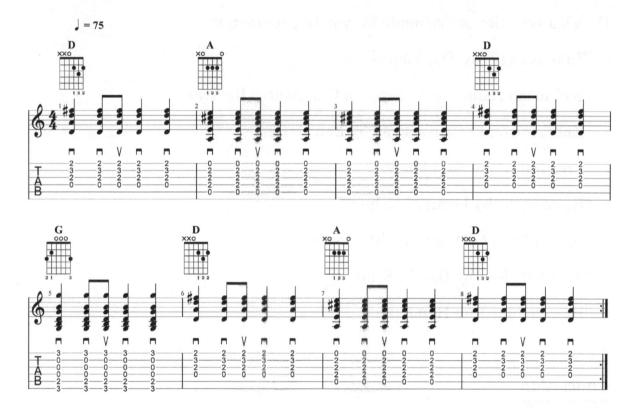

What Songs are Suitable for Beginners to Practice?

Although as a guitar player you might be tempted to learn the riffs and solos your heroes play; we have to build the foundations and walls before building a second floor and the roof. Therefore, when learning guitar, you should always focus on chords first.

In this sense, open chords are the easiest to learn and play, so songs utilizing these chords will be perfect to practice what you've learned while having fun.

Here's a selection we've made for you to get started:

» "Take it easy" by The Eagles

» "Bad moon rising" by Creedence Clearwater Revival

» "Knocking on heaven's door" by Bob Dylan

» "Free fallin'" by Tom Petty

» "Hallelujah" by Leonard Cohen

» "Brown Eyed Girl" by Van Morrison

» "Stand By Me" by Ben E. King

» "Hey Joe" by Jimi Hendrix

Conclusion

We have a lot more to learn, so I hope you join me in the lessons we have left on our ride.

Are you ready?

Let's do this!

Congratulations, you've made it through the first half of the book!

If you've followed every chapter, you should already be able to play simple guitar chord progressions. And that's a lot! With what you already know, you can play thousands of existing songs and thousands more to be composed (perhaps some by you?). It only takes looking at the chords and figuring out the song's rhythm.

There is an infinity of possible rhythms you can play on guitar, but the ones we've seen are the most common. Even if you encounter rhythmic patterns we haven't tried, with the experience you now have, you'll be able to figure them out with practice and patience.

Furthermore, the more you play, the easier it will be to figure out songs and rhythm patterns. Always remember that if you really want to play them perfectly, the metronome is your best friend when practicing!

Furthermore, if you think about the students of other instruments, you'll realize that the time it took you to learn the skills to play a thousand songs, is what takes it takes for violin players not to sound like an agonizing cat. Moreover, trombone players are still learning to blow a single note, and drummers... well, drummers are quick to learn how to make noise.

But, hey, I still have a lot to teach you because there are still many exciting things you can learn on guitar. We'll cover those in the second part of this book.

Arpeggios, power chords, capos, and other fun techniques with confusing names are waiting for you just a few pages away.

Let's go, your future as a great guitar player is just around the corner.

Let's do this!

PART 2

KEEP YOUR JOURNEY GOING

≡ CHAPTER 7 ≡

IT'S TIME FOR AN ITALIAN JOB; MEET MY FRIENDS THE ARPEGGIOS

Let's Talk Dynamics

In the past two weeks, you learned how to form chords and strum them by using single strokes to play most strings on your guitar. While that represents a high percentage of the guitar playing going on in the world, today we'll learn an alternative way of picking that can generate dynamics; one of the most important aspects of modern music.

But, what are arpeggios exactly? Is it a type of stuffed pasta you eat with Bolognese sauce? A sequel to The Sopranos? A Ferrari supercar model? Well, jokes apart, the word "arpeggio" does come from the Italian language but it means that, instead of playing most strings with single strokes, you'll be playing each string on its own.

Since it is a way of plucking the strings, it will be strictly a picking-hand technique that doesn't affect your fretting hand. Moreover, when you followed the checklist to play every chord correctly playing one string at a time, you were playing an arpeggio.

But why are arpeggios so important? Well, because they add dynamics to your playing without making things more complex for your fretting hand. How so? Well, for example, let's say that you are accompanying a singer with your guitar and the song has a quiet verse with an explosive chorus. You could create a sense of intimacy and make the song really small by playing the verse chords with an arpeggio and then strum them for the chorus allowing the song to "grow" in size and intensity.

Furthermore, this can be achieved without changing the chords, just by modifying your picking-hand technique.

So, as with other lessons in this book, chances are you'll be playing arpeggios on your guitar for a long time to come. Moreover, you can play the same chords that you know and they will sound very different.

Are you ready to conquer yet another skill and expand your guitar-playing catalog?

Go grab your guitar and get ready, we're going to have a great (Italian-flavored) time!

Creating Patterns with Arpeggios

Just like strumming patterns are ways to play a chord adding a rhythmic element to your music, arpeggios patterns repeat creating a hypnotic sequence of notes that gives texture and depth to any chord progression.

Arpeggio in 4/4

We'll get started with my favorite chord, the D chord. So, make a D chord with the fretting hand and use your picking hand to pluck each of the four strings in this chord in a descending pattern. This means you'll play the 4th string, then the 3rd string, the 2nd string after that, and finally the 1st string.

Once you've made it to the bottom string, repeat the sequence.

> **PRO TIP:** Always set up your metronome before practicing the exercises so you don't develop any bad rhythmic habits; they are really hard to get rid of later on, believe me. Also, for this first exercise, each string you pluck is a beat.

> It might a be a little hard to follow the textual instructions. Please refer to the audio track of this exercise before you begin to practice.

Arpeggio in 3/4

We'll use a different time signature for this exercise: 3/4. Just as a little refreshment of what we saw before, the time signature determines how many beats each bar has. In this case, instead of having 4 beats per bar, as we had before, we'll have only 3. So, instead of counting 1, 2, 3, 4, we'll count 1, 2, 3 per bar.

Famous songs that can be examples of this time signature are "The Times They are A-Changing" by Bob Dylan or "Nothing Else Matters" by Metallica. Also, it was the time signature of the romantic-era waltzes.

The way to play the exercise is exactly the same, going from one string to the next playing one note at a time with each beat.

> **PRO TIP:** Changing the time signature doesn't mean you need to stop using your metronome. On the opposite, you should change the time signature in your metronome of choice. Your tempo and sense of rhythm are an integral part of your playing; don't overlook them by creating healthy habits such as always (and I really mean always) practicing with a metronome.

Changing the Arpeggio Chord

As long as you keep your picking hand doing the same thing, you can create an arpeggio over any chord you feel like. So, we're going to try the same exercises with different time signatures but instead of playing them over a D chord, we'll do them over an A chord.

Since the 5th string when played open is the A note, we'll play strings 5 to 2 in descending order.

And once more, play four strings and then two back in 3/4 time signature.

Arpeggio Patterns in Chord Progressions

Now that you've statically played the chords, let's add some fretting-hand movement to these exercises and try arpeggio patterns changing the chords around a bit. I know what you're thinking, but don't worry, we'll stick to the chords you know so this will be more practice for the shapes you already know.

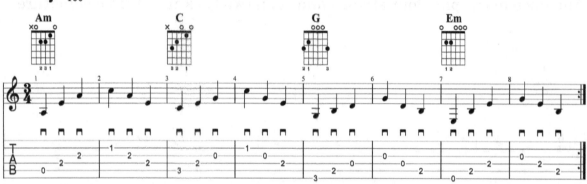

Sometimes arpeggios don't start from the lowest note of the chord. In this case, the right hand keeps playing the same strings, even if the lowest string used in the chord changes.

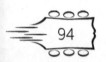

Conclusion

Good job with those arpeggios! Now you have another tool under your belt that you can use when playing all kinds of songs.

Arpeggios can add a lot of depth to your playing. The patterns we've seen are the easiest and most common, but they're already handy. Some guitar players can create otherworldly textures using arpeggios - and you will, too, if you practice enough.

Playing arpeggios is especially effective when you play with your picking-hand fingers instead of a pick, but that's out of the scope of this book. If you want to go deeper down that route, check our book on fingerstyle guitar. You'll learn how to create those unbelievably complex patterns using the chords we've learned in this book - the ones you already know! It's just about how you use your picking hand.

≡ CHAPTER 8 ≡

THE ALMIGHTY POWER CHORDS
(IT'S TIME FOR SOME DISTORTED GUITAR PLAYING!)

Introducing Power Chords, Rock's Middle Name

Power chords are the main resource for guitar players in many music styles like Punk, Rock, Metal, and many others. They are also called "5ths" because they are formed using the chord's root note and its fifth. Therefore, you'll see them written with a 5 next to the letter. For example, a D5 is a D power chord.

"Hey, hey, hey, not so fast Brainiac! What's all that mumbo jumbo?! Root note? Fifths?" Well, let me explain it to you in very simple terms.

Major and minor chords are "triads". This is a fancy word to say that they are built using three notes: the root note + the third + the fifth. This formula can be applied to every chord you've learned so far. So, for example, if you want to create a C chord you'll use the root note C plus the third, which is E, and the fifth, which is G.

But what happens if, instead of using a triad to play a chord, we use only the root note and the fifth, skipping the third? You might think that taking information out of the chord will make it sound smaller or dull; well, think again, because this formula focuses the listener's attention on a simpler formula which is great for fast chord changes, rocking riffs, and playing complicated songs in an uncomplicated way.

In other words, since the chord doesn't carry so much information, its effect on the listener is more powerful and makes everything more understandable. Therefore, the musical styles we talked about at the beginning, and with the right (obnoxious) amount of distortion, they create a "wall of sound".

A great example of this is the album Nevermind by Nirvana. All those hits are very simple to play and 90% of that record can be done using only power chords.

So, once again, power chords will help you broaden your scope and, if you want to play any rocking music style, they'll be your best, most powerful allies in getting a fierce, powerful, aggressive (even ferocious) sound from your guitar.

Are you ready to learn this powerful new skill and wow the world by playing gloriously fierce, epic power chords for screaming fans?

Get your guitar, because the power chord magic starts right now.

This is the Shape of Power

Remember when we were moving the same block or shape to create different chords like Am and E? Well, power chords, when played on the 6th and 5th string have the same shape allowing you to create any chord you want by simply moving the same shape from one fret to another.

This is the opposite of what we have been learning about open chords for which you need to remember a specific shape for each. In this case, we are going to learn a very simple formula that will allow us to move chord shapes from one place to another easily and effortlessly.

The formula is the following: your lowest note will give you the name of the chord while the fifth is always exactly two frets toward the guitar bridge in the following string. We will apply this same formula to make every power chord with its root note (the lowest note) in the 6th and 5th strings.

The E5 Chord

Let's get started the same way we started with open chords, playing the E chord. In this case, the E note is the open 6th string, therefore, to put together its power chord version we have to fret the fifth, which is always two frets to the bridge in the next string.

This is what the chord diagram looks like:

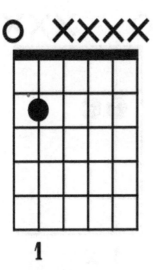

Check out the audio track in the bonus section to see how the E5 power chord sounds.

PRO TIP: Making the sound focused and tight is the name of the game when playing power chords. Therefore, you need to mute all the strings you're not playing when you strum. Remember, all you need is your root note and your 5th.

Power Chords with the Octave

Before moving on to another power chord, let's add another note to this shape so it sounds a little fuller and even bigger. The note we'll add is a repeated note because right in the string below the fifth, and in the same fret, we'll find the octave. The octave is the same note as the root note repeated one octave higher. This way, you're still playing the root and the 5th but repeating the root to make the chord sound even bigger and more epic.

This is what the chord diagram looks like with the added octave:

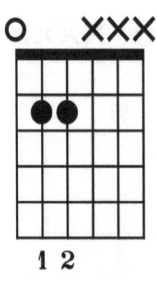

By the way, does this remind you of any other chord? These are the same notes as half of the Em chord we already knew!

The A5 Power Chord

To create the A5 chord, we just need to move the same structure we used for the E5 down a string and avoid playing our 6th string (remember that the root note for power chords is always the lower note played).

The G5 Power Chord

But what happens when the root note instead of being an open string is fretted? Well, we are going to use the same formula moving down the fretboard until we find the note we need. In this case, the note G is in the 6th string at the 3rd fret. That's exactly where our index will go. Then, we need to count two frets to the bridge and place our ring finger one string below. Therefore, our ring finger will go on the 5th string at the 5th fret.

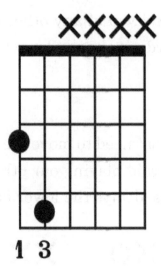

Now, if you feel your fingers a little tired, it is time to take a break before we move on to adding more chords to your vocabulary. Also, make sure you only play the top two strings and none of the other four.

Let's go through a little exercise in which we'll use this chord with a simple rhythm pattern. Close your eyes think of yourself as a punk rock star and use only downstrokes to make the rhythm more powerful and fierce.

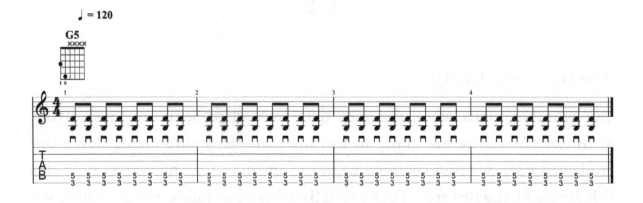

What about adding the octave to make this chord sound fuller? Well, that's very easy, the octave is exactly in the same place where it was with the E5 and A5 chords, right under the fifth. So, in this case, put your pinky in the 4th string at the 5th fret.

Now, we'll do the same but instead of using only downstrokes, we'll use down and up strokes.

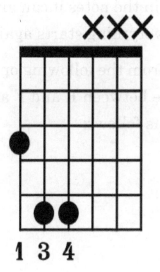

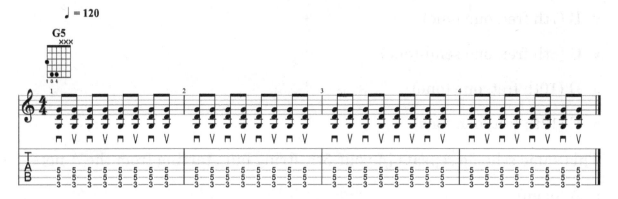

Forming Power Chords with your 6th and 5th String Root Notes

When we move the power chords as a block from one fret to another, we create different chords. Therefore, if we know where to find notes in the 6th and 5th strings, we can create any power chord we want.

So, your 6th string, when played open, is the E note. Every time you move one fret to the bridge, you move one semi-tone. You might be wondering what a semi-tone is. Well, it is the minimum distance between two notes.

We're going to get a little technical here, but I promise this will last no more than a couple of paragraphs and it will help you navigate the fretboard. Let's divide your 6th string in the notes it can give you from the open string until the 12th fret, where everything starts again.

So, all notes are separated from the following one by two semi-tones (or one tone) except for the distance between E and F and B and C. Therefore, the notes in your 6th string go as follows:

» E (open)

» F (1st fret, one semi-tone)

» G (3rd fret, one tone)

» A (5th fret, one tone

» B (7th fret, one tone)

» C (8th fret, one semi-tone)

» D (10th fret, one tone)

» E (12th fret, one tone)

This same scheme repeats in your 5th string but starting from the A note.

» A (open)

» B (2nd fret, one tone)

» C (3rd fret, one semi-tone)

» D (5th fret, one tone)

» E (7th fret, one tone)

» F (8th fret, one semi-tone)

» G (10th fret, one tone)

» A (12th fret, one tone)

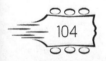

So, if you follow this scheme you can create any power chord you want.

> **PRO TIP:** As you've just seen, power chords can be played in more than one position, the one that you find more comfortable to move to. For example, you can play the A5 chord with the open string as you've seen before, or on the 6th string at the 5th fret. Economizing movements is the secret to quick and smooth chord changes.

Power Chord Exercises with Chord Changes

Let's try to apply all of this in the following exercises. Remember, you can look for the chord you want to play at the position it is more convenient for you.

OK! That was a wrap for the day ; we learned a lot, didn't we? Well, give those fingers a rest because tomorrow we'll practice a lot and find some new power chords!

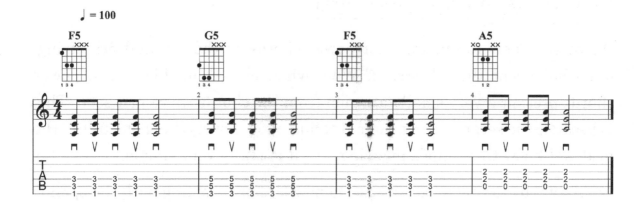

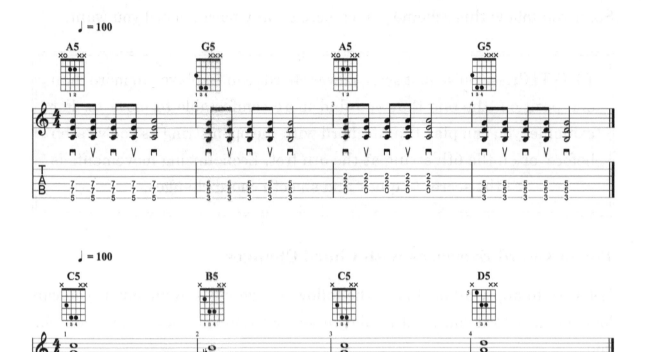

Power Chords Starting on the 4th String

We've seen how to put together power chords in the 6th and 5th string, but what about the 4th string? Well, when played on this string, power chords present a very small variation from the chords we've just seen. This is because the second string, your B string, moves everything one fret to the bridge. I know this sounds puzzling, but it is really very simple.

Let's start by taking a look at the D5 power chord starting with the open D string adding the fifth (two frets to the left, one string below) and the octave which will not be under the fifth, but one more fret to the bridge.

The chord diagram looks like this:

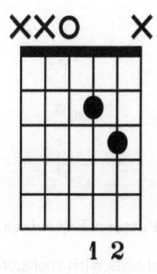

So, what happens if we want to move from the D5 to the E5 power chord moving the entire block? Well, very simply we just use the same formula and put our index finger on the 4th string at the 2nd fret, the ring finger on the 3rd string at the 4th fret, and the pinky at the 5th fret on the 2nd string.

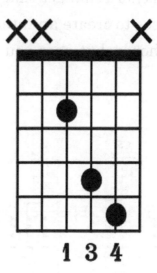

Exercise with Power Chords on the 4th String

Now, using the same formula we learned yesterday, let's play these exercises using only 4th-string power chords.

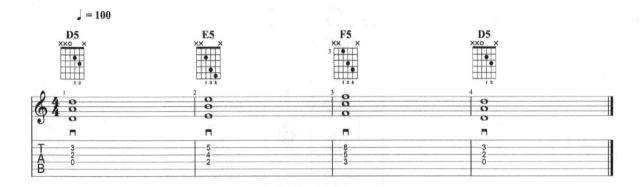

Power Chord & Rhythm Pattern Exercises

Now that we've seen power chords with root notes on the top three strings, it is time to mix them up a little and add some rhythm patterns to them.

Exercise 1

This is a very simple series of chord changes that will help you move the same structure only small distances to create an interesting chord progression. I know it looks like a lot of chords, but once you play it, you'll realize it is a very simple exercise.

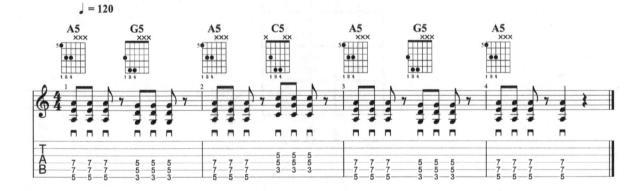

Exercise 2

To finish this series of exercises, let's use the omnipresent rhythm pattern we learned in chapter 5 with a power chord progression. It looks like this:

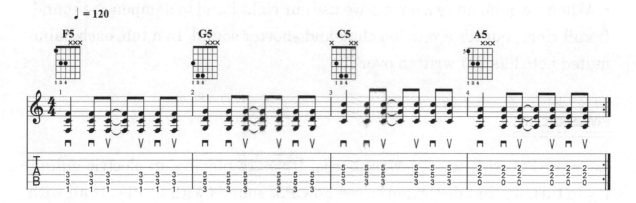

Getting Really Menacing with Palm-Muting Techniques

Palm mute (abbreviated as PM) is a right-hand technique that allows you to create a muffled and more percussive sound. It's often used with either single notes or power chords.

When played on an electric guitar with distortion, it creates a thick sound commonly used in Rock/Metal and similar genres. But PM can also be played without distortion (on any kind of guitar) to create a subdued and percussive sound that works well in accompanying other instruments.

To palm mute, do a karate chop on your guitar bridge. Not a real one (unless you have a replacement guitar), but the idea is to place the side of your palm on it while holding the pick. Keep the hand there, finger an Em chord with your picking hand, and experiment with plucking the strings. The sound should be close to a bass-driven "chug" sound and it should also be much shorter than usual.

Keep in mind that palm muting is not the same as muting the string:

» When we mute a string, we use our left hand to prevent it from ringing. In a tab, each muted note is written with an x.

» When we palm mute a string, we use our right hand to dampen the sound. It still rings, but it's a muffled chug and shorter sound. In a tab, each palm-muted note has PM written over it.

PM exercises

Let's try PM with some power chords. If you're playing an electric guitar, try to turn up that distortion to see how PM sounds with it. Play it all with downstrokes.

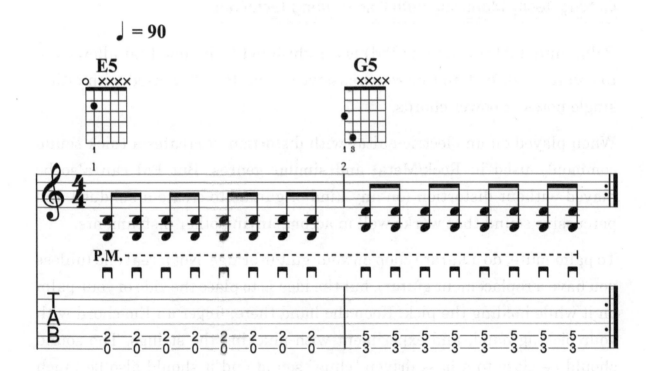

Now try to play this one with downstrokes and upstrokes. Upstrokes with power chords can be tricky at first, but they'll allow you to play fast more comfortably.

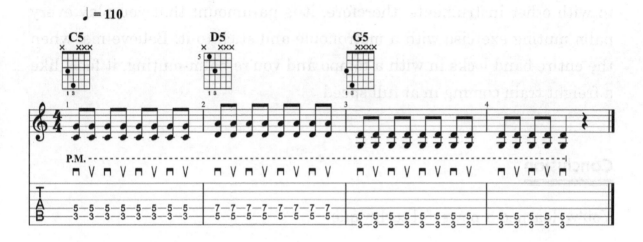

PM notes and two-string power chords with three-string power chords let us create exciting rhythms full of contrasts.

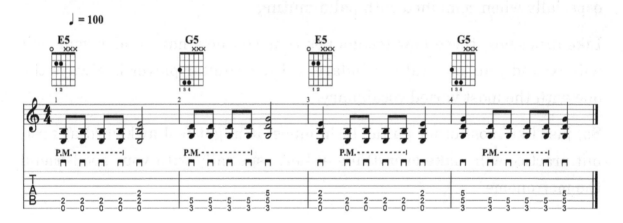

Points to consider

» Remember how, with open chords, we generated dynamics on open chords? Well, strumming and palm muting alternately generates dynamics when playing distorted power chords. For example, you can create a heavy

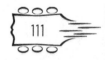

contrast between verse and chorus. A great example of this is the song "Hash Pipe" by Weezer.

» When playing muted power chords in the real world, you'll probably lock in with other instruments, therefore, it is paramount that you play every palm muting exercise with a metronome and stick to it. Believe me, when the entire band locks in with a tempo and you're palm-muting, it feels like a freight train coming in at full speed.

Conclusion

You've learned a powerful technique!

Power chords on a distorted electric guitar are the bread and butter of electric guitar players playing the most aggressive music genres. That being said, they can also be used on the acoustic guitar to create rhythmic patterns, especially when combined with palm muting.

Like arpeggios, these new techniques that you now have under your belt will expand your musical vocabulary. A better guitar player is always the one with the most varied vocabulary.

So, just like most other guitar techniques, it might feel awkward at first, but practice will make everything easier; especially with your good friend the metronome.

≡ CHAPTER 9 ≡

THE TENSION-MAKERS, MEET THE SEVENTH CHORDS!

Raise the Feeling With These Chords!

Let me introduce you to my most dramatic friends: the seventh chords. If Mr. Metronome was the king of tempo, they are the drama kings of the music world.

We've seen major, minor, and power chords. We also learned that the major and minor chords are formed using triads and that the power chords only need the root and the fifth. Well, the seventh chords are formed utilizing 4 notes instead of 3 (or 2).

They are very commonly found in styles like jazz and blues but can also be the ace up the sleeve of other genres like pop, rock, funk, and more. I mean an ace up the sleeve because they are perfect to create tension, and hooks, and to add layers of complexity to any simple chord progression.

Moreover, seventh chords have the particularity of creating tension that begs to be resolved, and the way we solve that tension is by playing a specific major chord. That tension-release interplay is the heart and soul of most hit songs you love. That is because seventh chords will get your attention, elevate your tension, and then resolve it with a major chord that will put a smile on your face.

This is close to what we have been talking about regarding the feelings that chords create.

» Major chords are happy and full and work great for choruses.

» Minor chords are sad and darker and work amazing for verses.

» Seventh chords elevate tension that begs to be resolved and make amazing bridges.

The "bridge" of a song is the segment that leads you from a verse into the chorus, in case you didn't know. Although it is very common, it is nowhere nearly as popular as verses and choruses are.

Are you ready to add another chord type to your musical vocabulary and elevate the game?

Well, go get your guitar because there is a lot of playing coming your way!

> **PRO TIP:** Seventh chords are new shapes you need to learn. If at the beginning you come across one and you don't remember its shape, you can simply swap it by its major version and it will sound OK. Maybe not as well and you'll miss the tension-raising effect, but it won't sound odd or like a mistake

Getting Started: The A7 and E7 Chords

Just with a quick glance, you'll realize that the shape of the E7 and A7 chords is very similar to the major version of these chords. That being said, since a major chord is a triad (three notes) and the seventh chords are quartets (four notes) there will always be one changing note.

For example, to play the E7 chord all you need to do is add a note with your pinky and for the A7 you have to lift your middle finger to let that open G ring instead of pressing at the second fret to create an A.

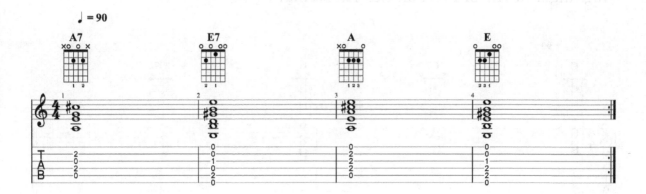

The D7 Chord

To create a D7 chord in your guitar you have to do something close to what you did with the A7 chord and instead of fretting the 2nd string at the 3rd fret, you'll finger it at the 1st fret turning that D note into a C.

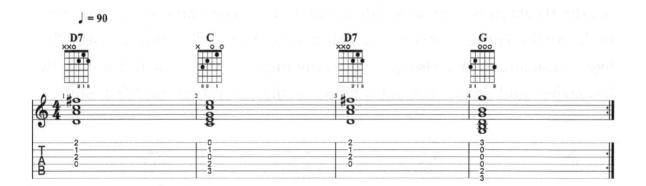

You can practice the above progression by following along to the audio track available in the bonus section

Moving on, the C7 and G7 Chords

To create a C7 chord, you have to add a note to it placing your pinky at the 3rd fret on the 3rd string. Likewise, to play a G7 chord, you have to add your ring finger at the 3rd fret on the 4th string.

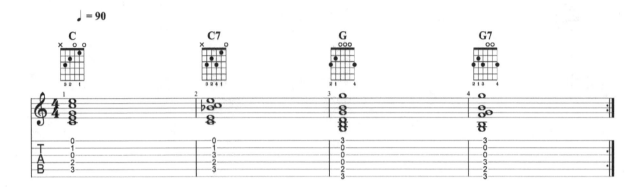

Introducing the B7 Chord

B is a chord that we haven't seen so far other than in power chords. This isn't an act of discrimination or because we don't like its sound, but because it's a difficult chord to finger. Worry not, though, because we'll see more than one version of it later on.

So, the B7 chord isn't at all a difficult chord to finger; you need to place your pinky at the 2nd fret on the 1st string, and your middle finger at the 2nd fret on the 5th string. Also, put your ring finger at the same fret but on the 3rd string, and finally, the index finger at the 1st fret on the 4th string.

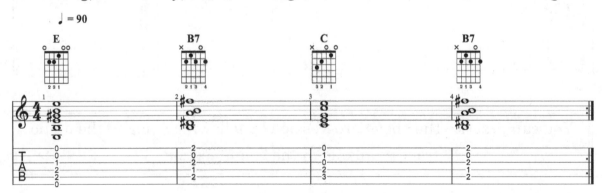

Introducing the Chord of Love, Meet the Major Seventh Chords

The Major Seventh chords are not major and are not seventh chords. Therefore, if we have, for example, the A chord, we can turn it into:

» The A major chord (A)

» The A seventh chord (A7)

» The A major seventh chord (Amaj7)

All these are variations of the same chord that can be used in different scenarios to generate different dynamics, feelings, and textures.

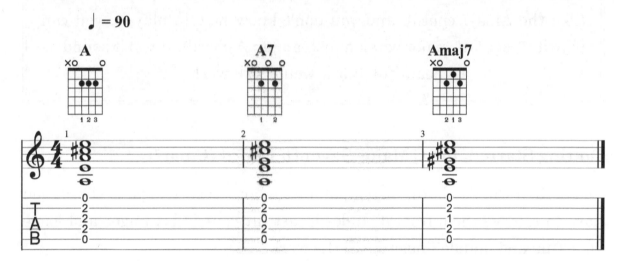

I know. Couldn't we have chosen a less confusing way to name them? But hey, don't blame it on us; this has been the chord's name for centuries!

Oh, the major 7th chord!

They say the music genius Frank Zappa used to call it the "falling in love chord." This is because it has a complex and beautiful yet delicate sound. And it can easily sound Jazzy.

In many ways, they're the opposite of power chords. While the simplicity of power chords makes them work well with loud distortion, the complexity and delicacy of Maj7 chords make them work better for softer playing.

Even without distortion, Maj7 chords don't work well everywhere. Their complex sound can feel out of place in genres of popular music that benefit from simplicity. That being said, they can also be the single turn that makes a song more compelling. Therefore, knowing them (and broadening your vocabulary as a player) will make you a better guitarist.

> **PRO TIP:** Just like with 7th chords, if you encounter a maj7 chord (like the Amaj7 chord), and you don't know how to play it, you can play its "regular" major version instead (an A chord). It won't sound as beautiful, but it would still work.

Getting Started, the C Major Seventh Chord (Cmaj7)

To create a Cmaj7 chord, instead of adding any fingers to your chord, you have to remove them from it. Indeed, just lift your index finger and leave your ring and middle finger do all the work.

You'll notice that the sounds from the next exercise could very well belong to a jazz song.

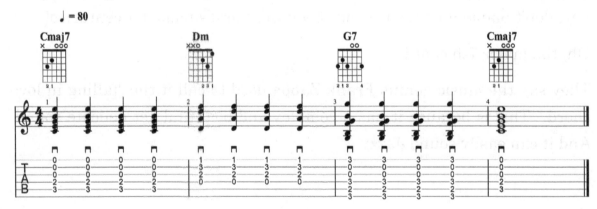

Major Seventh Chords & Arpeggios, a Match Made in Heaven

Some complex chords can be enjoyed much more when we take time to digest them sonically in all their intricate glory. Therefore, playing them one string at a time is the perfect way to let the romantic and multifaceted structure of major seventh chords shine through and haunt the listener.

Let's try it in this exercise with the Amaj7 and Dmaj7 chords.

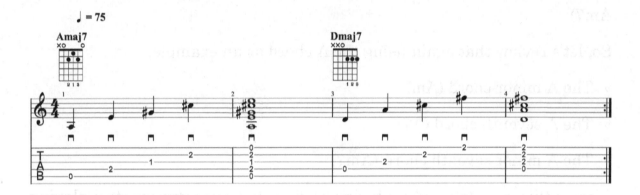

FAQ : How Do I Memorize All Chord Shapes?

There aren't many shortcuts in guitar playing but there is one that is very useful when you're trying to learn all chord shapes by heart. Certainly, the perfect way to do it is by learning the changes between chords.

So, for example, let's say that you're playing an Am chord. From that shape, you can make another chord moving just one finger. You can move your ring finger to the 5th string at the 3rd fret and you'll make a C major. Also, you can move your index finger to the 4th string, at the 2nd fret, and your middle and ring fingers down to create an A major chord. Finally, removing the middle finger will get you an A7 too. The list can go on and on, but it is up to you to complete it now.

So, take your time and try different combinations. Once you learn several changes between chords, you won't have to think about entire shapes but the movement of one or two fingers.

Introducing the Sad Tension Raisers: Minor Seventh Chords

Seventh chords can be divided into three categories: seventh chords (like A7), major seventh chords (like Amaj7), and minor seventh chords (like Am7).

So, let's review that again using the A chord as an example:

» The A minor chord (Am)

» The A seventh chord (A7)

» The A minor seventh chord (Am7)

I know this sounds a tad confusing at first, but once you practice playing them, you'll be able not only to tell the difference between them but also understand where they can be used to create the biggest impact.

Getting Started, The Em7 and Am7 Chords

Let's see two minor 7th chords: Em7 and Am7. As it happened with E7 and A7, they're very similar to the original E and A, but made by removing one of your fingers, creating a "hole" in the chord.

Let's see them in an exercise so you can start getting familiarized with how they sound.

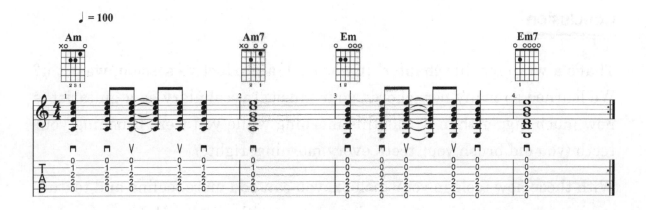

Chords Salad, Mixing Flavors Up!

Let's try minor seventh chords next to other chords. In this case, keep the index finger on string 2 when you change from the Am7 to the D7 chord. Also, you can finger the Em7 chord with the middle finger instead of the index finger. This way, you'll already have that finger ready for the following E7.

Remember, looking for ways to minimize finger movement makes playing everything much easier!

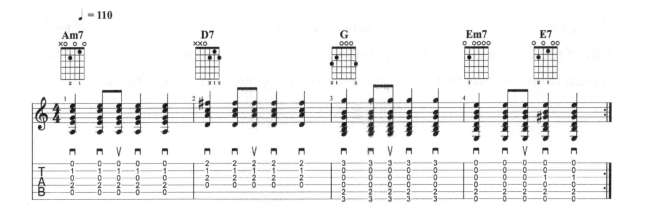

Conclusion

That's a wrap for this chapter! It was such a productive session, wasn't it? We learned so many new chords your musical vocabulary as a guitarist is now much bigger than it was this morning while you were brushing your teeth (you did brush your teeth every morning, right?).

With these new tools in your toolbox, you can add more feeling and texture to your playing making it more interesting with enhanced dynamics. In a nutshell, learning more chords and expanding your vocabulary will make you a better, more complete, and versatile player. Furthermore, when you write your own music, you can add more flavors and texture which will draw people in.

Finally, as you probably noticed throughout the chapter, the fact that a chord sounds more complex doesn't necessarily mean it is more complex to play. On the opposite, the Am7 chord is easier to play than the A chord, right? Therefore, the sound of your guitar can be inviting and haunting effortlessly.

Well, get some rest and let all this info sink in because the next chapter is full of guitar playing, fun, and lots of learning. I'll introduce you to another friend of mine that works wonders to playing with singers: The capo.

≡ CHAPTER 10 ≡

USING A CAPO TO EXPAND YOUR GUITAR'S POSSIBILITIES

Why Should You Learn How To Use a Capo?

A capo is a very handy guitar accessory that allows you to move the guitar nut (the little white or black piece strings go through to get to the tuners) to any fret you need to.

You might be frowning now and thinking "but why is that something useful?" Well, the answer to that question is very simple, you can play new, different chords in the same open positions you've learned.

That's right, if you, for example, position the capo on your guitar's neck at the 1st fret, it will press down all the strings at the same time. Therefore, for example, plucking your open 6th string will no longer generate an E but an F. Likewise, if you play the same shape of an E chord, it will turn into an F chord. In the same vein, placing the capo at your third fret will turn your E chord shape into a G chord.

This repeats with every string and every open chord shape you've learned so far.

In What Situations Can a Capo Become Useful?

These are some of the scenarios in which using a capo on your guitar can save the day:

» **Playing with a singer** – Guitars are an infinite canvas for creation because, as long as you can fret it and pluck it, you can play any note. The human voice, on the other hand, can cover a certain range. Therefore, if you sing, or play with a singer, you can accommodate a song to suit 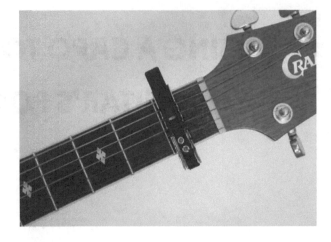 your voice or your singer's voice by using a capo and moving the structure upper on the fretboard.

» For example, if you accompany a female singer and want to play an Elvis Presley cover, you can move it "up" in pitch until the singer finds it comfortable. Then, just play the same chord shapes you would without the capo.

» **Playing a song in its original pitch** – Capos are widely used not only live but in the studio as well. Therefore, if you want to play a song just like it was recorded, you can use a capo as the band did. For example, "Wonderwall" by Oasis was recorded with a capo at the 2nd fret and "Tumbling Dice" by the Rolling Stones with a capo at the 4th fret.

» **Creating new sounds** – Placing your capo after the 5th fret, you can get your guitar to sound close to a mandolin. Furthermore, you can capo your guitar as far high as the 12th fret. A great example of this technique is The Beatles' megahit "Here Comes the Sun". George Harrison used a capo at the 7th fret to create that iconic sound. Also, players like The Tallest Man on

Earth use this technique along with alternate tunings to come up with new, original, and inspiring sounds.

How Does It Work? Going from Theory to Practice

Let's get started with the following chord progression: Em - D - G - A7.

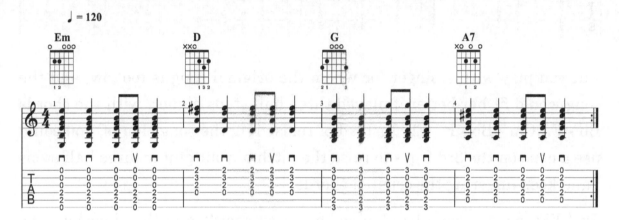

Refer to the audio track of the above progression to follow along

Using a capo at the 1st fret, you'll get Fm - Eb - Ab - Bb7. Moreover, moving it one fret, using it at the 2nd fret, you'll get F#m - E - A - B7. Finally, if you make a bold move and use it at the 7th fret, you'll get Bm - A - D - E7.

So, if you have a capo, try to play it with the capo in those positions to see how it changes the sound.

A Capo Spotted in the Wild

Now, imagine a real-life situation. Let's say you're playing a chord progression we've seen before, the one from "Knockin' on Heaven's Door" By Bob Dylan. The chords are G - D - Am - G - D - C.

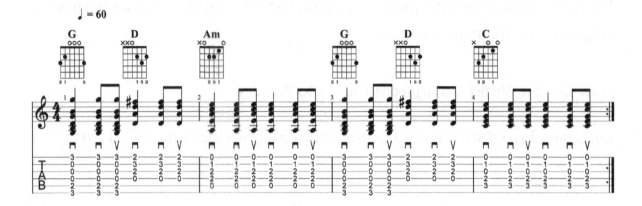

But you play with a singer for whom the original song is too low, and the song would fit her better if played three half steps higher, with the chords Bb - F - Cm - Bb - F - Eb. Instead of relearning the song chords, you could use a capo on the 3rd fret - to raise the pitch of your guitar three half steps - and keep fingering the original chords.

Just like magic, you'll be playing the same chords and the singer will be singing in a more comfortable pitch!

If you're unsure about the right pitch for a singer (or yourself), try playing the same chords with the capo in different positions and see what works best.

On what fret should I use the capo?

To know what fret you should place the capo on, we first need to go through a super brief music theory lesson. This will work as a refresher and expand on what we saw in chapter 8 when we saw power chords.

Ready? Let's do this!

In music, there are 12 possible notes:

A - A#/Bb - B - C - C#/Db - D - D#/Eb - E - F - F#/Gb - G - G#/Ab

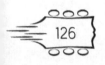

Many notes can be named in two different ways. A# is the same as Bb, and D# is the same as Eb.

The distances between notes are called half steps or semi-tones, and two half steps equal one whole step or a tone. The A note is a half-step away from A#/Bb and two half-steps (or one whole step) away from B. So, from C to G, there are seven half steps (or three-and-a-half whole steps).

Chords are made of notes and work in the same way. An A chord is a half-step away from an A# chord (or a Bb chord, which is identical). Also, a C chord is seven half-steps away from a G chord.

On guitar, each fret equals a half-step of distance. As you already know, when you play the string 6 open, you're playing an E. When you play the same string but press the 1st fret, you're playing a note that's a half step higher, an F. When you press the 3rd fret, you're playing three half steps higher than E; a G.

In the same way, your fingers do, a capo will rise half steps equal to the number of the fret you put it on. If you want to raise the pitch of all your chords a half step, place the capo at the 1st fret. If you want to rise it four half steps, place the capo at the 4th fret. And so on.

This table shows what chords you would produce with each fingered chord depending on the fret you place the capo.

Open chord shape	Capo 3rd fret	Capo 2nd fret	Capo 3rd fret	Capo 4th fret	Capo 5th fret	Capo 6th fret	Capo 7th fret
C	C# Db	D	D# Eb	E	F	F# Gb	G
A	A# Bb	B	G	C# Db	D	D# Eb	E
Am	A#m Bbm	Bm	Gm	C#m Dbm	Dm	D#m Ebm	Em
G	G# Ab	A	A# Bb	B	C	C# Db	D
E	F	F# Gb	G	G# Ab	A	A# Bb	B
Em	Fm	F#m Gbm	Gm	G#m Abm	Am	A#m Bbm	Bm
D	D# Eb	E	F	F# Gb	G	G# Ab	A
Dm	D#m Ebm	Em	Fm	F#m Gbm	Gm	G#m Abm	Am

It might seem confusing at first, but it will become easy once you interiorize the concept. Come back to this table whenever you're unsure where to place the capo.

That is a wrap for this chapter; we learned a lot!

Go get some rest that you'll need for what is coming next; I have another surprise waiting for you... and you're going to love it!

Class dismissed!

Conclusion

A capo can be wonderfully useful and save you a lot of headaches, especially when you sing or play with a singer. It's not uncommon for beginner singers to think they don't have a good voice when the problem is that they simply weren't playing songs that fit their vocal range. The capo is an easy solution to this problem since it lets you find the right pitch without learning any new chords.

Other times you might want to play songs that have been composed to be played with a capo. And sometimes, you might just want to experiment with higher-pitch guitar sounds. For each of these scenarios, having a capo and knowing how to use it is paramount.

There's only one caveat to keep in mind: the capo can only raise the pitch of your guitar and not lower it. If you want to lower the guitar's pitch, you can tune it down (up to one whole step). However, this takes longer to prepare than simply placing a capo on the fretboard.

Regardless of how often you use capo, keeping one at hand is a good idea. You never know when you'll need it.

≡ CHAPTER 11 ≡

CHORD PROGRESSIONS, SONGS & MORE FUN!

Using All Our Tools to Make Magic Happen

We've been putting tool after tool inside our box and now it's time to make use of all of them to make musical magic happen.

I told you that I had another surprise for you; well, I'm a man of my word and the surprise comes in the shape of some of my favorite songs (that can surely become your favorites too). Yes, we're going to have lots of fun today practicing trying to mimic the style that made us love our heroes.

Before we get started with the fun, though, there are some recommendations I need to make:

» **Play them with a metronome** – I know we are having fun but when the fun comes with a lesson it becomes twice as good. Therefore, I've written down the bpm in every exercise. As a pro tip, try playing it slow and perfectly, and then work on your speed.

» **New strumming patterns** – You'll find some new strumming patterns in the upcoming exercises. Don't freak out when you see them, we've gone the extra mile and made a recording to help you figure them out. Yeah, I know, you're welcome.

In The Style of "Guns n' Roses"

Sweet Child O' Mine by Guns n' Roses is one of those songs you've probably heard so many times you know every word of it by heart. Well, in this exercise we'll learn the verse chords so you can sing those lyrics as many times as you see fit.

> **PRO TIP:** The chord progression is utterly simple. Yet, the rhythm pattern requires you to pay special attention to your picking hand. So, focus on that hand and try to follow the recording until you can nail chords and rhythm.

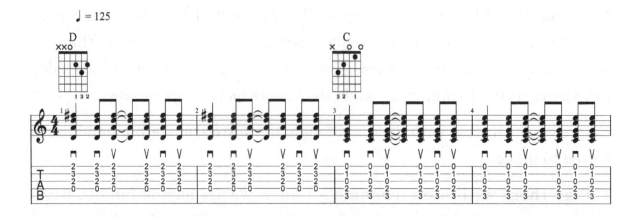

> Play the audio track available in the bonus section, focus on rhythm and try to keep up!

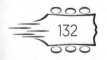

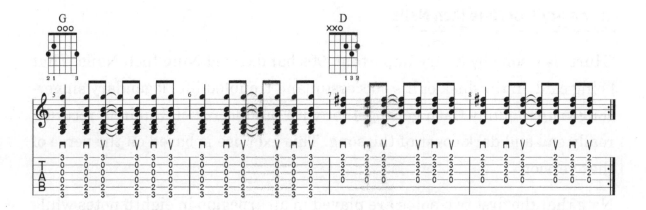

In The Style of Bart Howard

This is a jazz standard written by Bart Howard in 1954 and later popularized by Frank Sinatra. Although you'll find a zillion versions of it, Mr. Sinatra's voice adds a velvet touch that makes it irresistible. And yes, we're going to learn how to play it.

You'll notice a very interesting blend of seventh, minor seventh, and major seventh chords that create a complex atmosphere. Opposite to the last exercise, try to focus on your fretting hand since the rhythm pattern is very minimalistic; it's only quarter notes played with downstrokes.

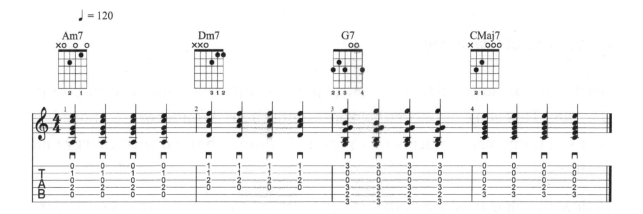

In The Style of Nine Inch Nails

"Hurt" is a song by a very important '90s band called Nine Inch Nails. That being said, in the dusk of his successful and troubled life, legendary singer-songwriter Johnny Cash got together with producer Rick Rubin to record a really sad and dark cover of the song. This exercise is based on the verse of that version.

Note that the first two notes are played in an arpeggio in eighth notes while the last three beats are the chord played with a single downstroke. If this hybrid approach feels daunting, follow the recording and you'll be making your audience weep in no time.

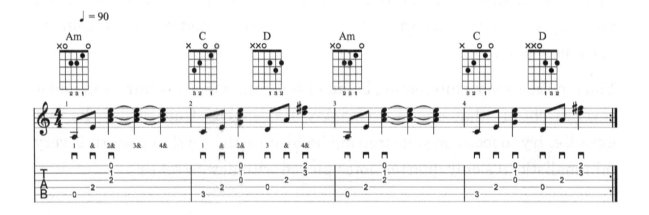

In The Style of Green Day

Green Day is, arguably, the most popular punk rock band to come up in the '90s. This song in particular represents their "Wonderwall". Indeed, it is one of their very few acoustic songs and is supercharged with energy and positive vibes.

Follow the chords of the verse and pay attention to the particular rhythm pattern. As a word of warning, it is likely you won't stop singing it in your head for at least a week!

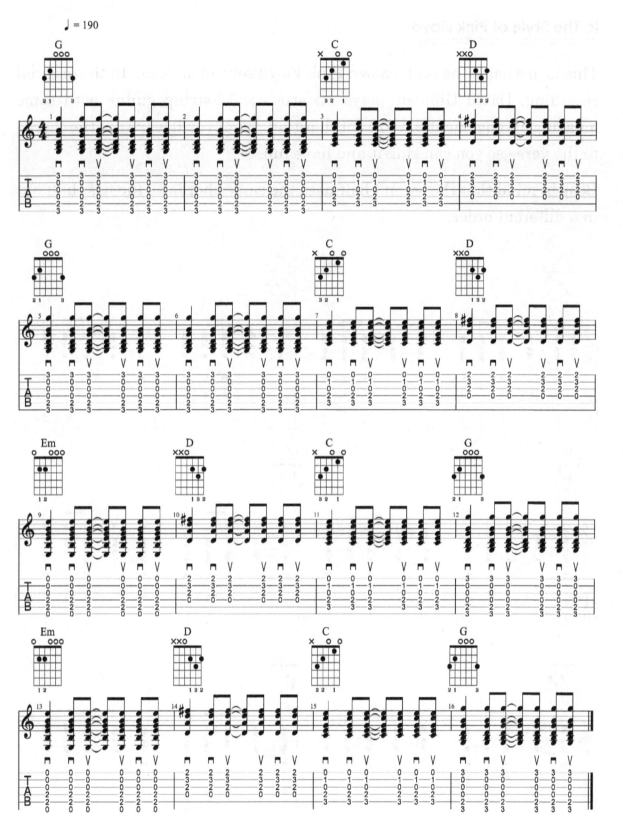

In The Style of Pink Floyd

This is, perhaps, the best-known Pink Floyd song of all time. In the original recording, David Gilmour plays an acoustic 12-string guitar with some amazing arrangements. We're not there yet. What you'll learn are the chords to the verse so you can sing it and have fun.

Bear in mind that the second half uses the same chords as the first half but in a different order.

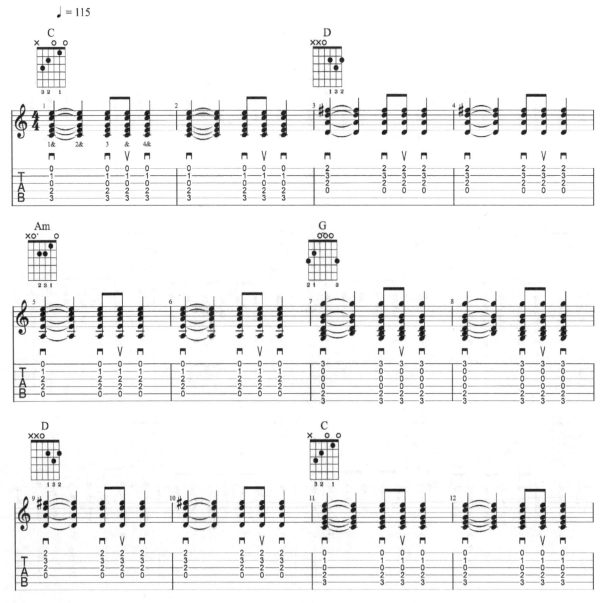

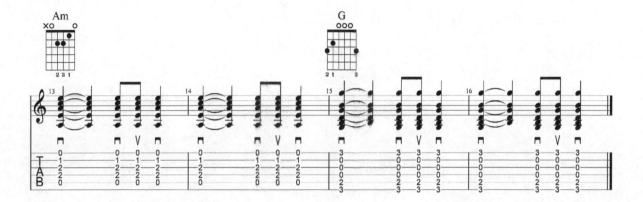

Conclusion

That's a wrap for this chapter!

Great job with these chord progressions! I hope you loved my song selection as much as I loved putting it together for you. Remember, the more you play, the better you'll play. Moreover, you'll improve even faster if you practice with a metronome.

We're heading toward the last chapter which is paramount for your successful career as a guitar player. So, before finishing our journey together, I'd like you to learn how to play chords which are a crucial stepping stone for all guitarists on the planet. Furthermore, these chords are a before and after for every guitarist.

Yes, you probably guessed; I'm talking about... bar chords!

So, get some proper rest because what comes up next is the final chapter of the book; and we'll end on a very high note.

≡ CHAPTER 12 ≡

BAR CHORDS, THE FINAL FRONTIER

Getting Started; Bar Chords? What are those!?

Bar chords get their name from the position your index finger adopts when playing them. Remember we talked about how a capo could be placed over all strings and move the nut of the guitar further down the fretboard? Well, our index finger will form a bar that will press all strings the same way. The big difference is that it isn't static, you can move it around freely.

You might be scratching the top of your head with your pick and thinking: "Didn't I just spend days learning all chords? What do I need to learn bar chords for!?"

Let me break down the benefits of playing bar chords for you.

To begin with, a bar chord is something you can consider a mix between an open chord and a power chord. How so? Well, very simple: you can move the same shape around the fretboard and, as long as you know what note is the lowest your index finger frets, you'll be able to play any chord you like. Just like we did with power chords, remember? If not, make a small pause and go back to chapter 8.

But wait, because there is more. You can move the same shape around the neck and create major chords, minor chords, seventh chords, and minor seventh chords. Moreover, since you always play at least 5 strings, they sound full and strong like an open chord that you can move around easily.

Finally, these two benefits combined allow you to learn just a handful of shapes and create any chord you need with them at any given time. This will simplify your playing drastically.

Yes, bar chords aren't the easiest at the beginning, but believe me, learning them is worth every single drop of energy you invest in them. They will help you become a much better guitar player and can save you from more than one moment your brain decides to go blank about an open chord shape and to make fast and smooth changes between chords.

Are you ready to learn this final skill and grow even more as a guitarist?

Go get your guitar because here we go!

Learning the Almighty F Chord

The F chord is an elusive one because it's hard to play it on the guitar fretting the right triad. Indeed, we, guitar players, are always constrained by shapes and distances. If you were playing, let's say, a piano, the F chord would be just another chord.

Therefore, we'll work our way there through alternate, simpler shapes until we can fret a full F major chord as a proper bar chord. If it seems very hard, especially at the beginning, don't get discouraged, with some practice you'll be able to play it effortlessly shortly.

The F5 Chord (Or Half the F Chord)

You already know how to create an F5 or an F power chord. We'll use the version we learned with an extra octave and play only the top 3 strings.

Get the sonic reference of the F5 chord by playing the audio track available in the bonus section

Moving on, Let's Add One Finger

Add the middle finger on the 3rd string at the 2nd fret to the same chord you have already fretted. This will get you very close to what an F major sounds like when played as a bar chord. The big difference is that you're still not fretting or playing the 2nd and 1st strings.

As you'll see (and hear) later on, this is not a minor detail by any means. So, either refrain from plucking them or mute them with the lower part of your index finger.

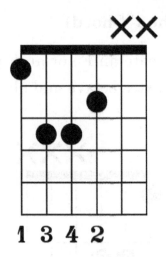

You don't have to strum strings 1 and 2 with this chord, and I recommend using your index finger to touch them slightly so that they don't ring. And you've got your first F chord! This isn't a proper bar chord yet, but it's similar.

Let's try it in action

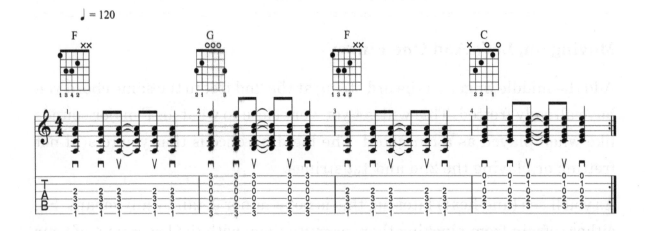

The Cheating-With-The-Thumb Technique

Remember back in the first chapter of this book I told you that guitar virtuoso John Mayer and legend Jimi Hendrix used their larger-than-life thumbs to fret the 6th string? Well, the time has come to steal their trick and use it to our convenience.

So, try moving your palm up until it touches the guitar neck and fret the 6th string at the 1st fret with your thumb. Does it feel awkward or very hard? Don't worry; I have good news for you. If you can actually fret the note, even if it buzzes or doesn't sound great at the beginning, you're part of the little percentage of guitar players who can pull this off physically. The rest of us just don't have a thumb big enough.

Practice, practice, practice, and once you've mastered this technique, practice some more.

The chord chart looks like this (the "T" is for thumb):

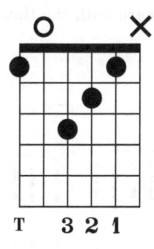

In this version of the F chord, you can let open string 5 ring. It's ok if you accidentally mute it with the thumb; the chord will still sound good!

We don't play string 1 here, and you can mute it with the index finger, so you don't have to worry about not strumming that string. However, if we do let it ring, this F evolves into a beautiful version of a Fmaj7 chord:

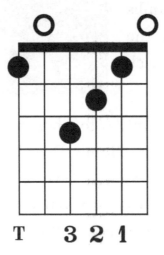

Let's play the same progression as before, but playing the F chords with the thumb and turning the second one into a Fmaj7. Notice how it's easy to change from this Fmaj7 to C - you can keep the index down while moving the middle and ring fingers to the following strings.

If you can't reach the fretboard with the thumb, just skip this exercise; there's plenty more to come!

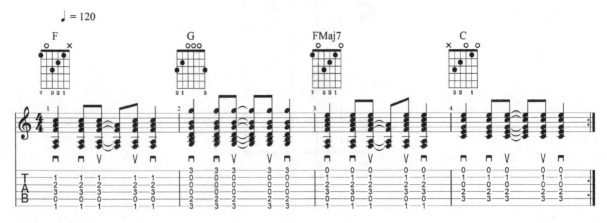

The Full F Bar Chord

OK, the moment has come; this is a pivotal time in your playing career: you'll play your first bar chord in a matter of minutes. It's like when you felt the plane speeding up on the track before take-off the first time you ever flew.

I won't lie, it is hard and it takes time and practice to do it right, but let me also stress it's worth every second of time.

To begin with, place your fingers in the shape of the F chord as we've seen before, and try to fret the 2nd and 1st string with the index finger.

Let me give you two tips that can help you make this a little easier:

1. Roll your finger slightly so that the outer side of your finger is what frets the strings. This is because there is less meat in that part of your finger than the part that goes from the tip to the palm.

Therefore, with your bone closer to the skin, your finger is harder and flatter there. This way, you won't have to make such an effort to make strings sound.

2. This is kind of a continuation of something you saw in the first chapter. The strength to make strings sound properly in a bar chord doesn't come from your index finger but from the muscles between the thumb and the index.

As we said at the beginning, it will take time to build strength in that muscle so take it easy and go slowly.

Start by fingering the half F chord we've seen earlier. Make sure all strings ring well.

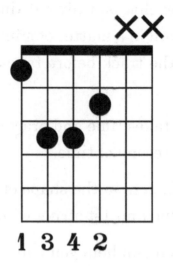

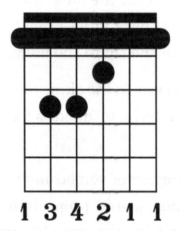

This is tricky, and making all strings sound clearly at first will be hard. But with practice and patience, you'll get better at it. It's a tiring position until your fingers develop more strength, so take breaks and stop immediately if you feel any pain. There's no rush in learning this; we already know other ways of playing the F chord, so take it easy!

If you feel ready, let's test this F bar chord:

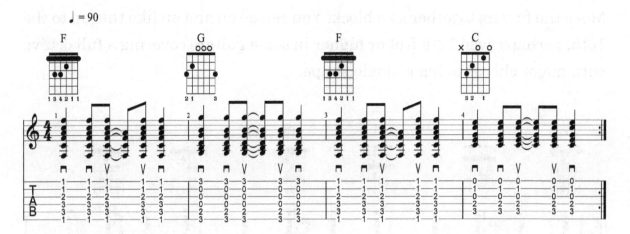

To the F Bar Chord and Beyond

Great! I'm sure it's still tough to finger this chord, but mastering it will take your playing to a new level.

The best part of learning the F bar chord is that you can play many other major chords using the same fingering on different frets. You simply have to move all fingers at once, as a block, one or more frets higher.

You can go back to Chapter 8 and take a look at the notes and frets we saw for power chords because bar chords follow the same guide. Moreover, you can also refer to the chart we saw in the capo chapter to add sharps and flats to the equation.

Therefore, for example, if you finger an F bar chord and move it one fret higher, you'll get an F# chord (also named Gb). If you move yet another fret further, you'll get a G major bar chord. One more, and you get a G# (aka Ab), and so on.

Bar Chords in Ascending Sequence

Let's try playing bar chords as you would in the real world with this exercise. You'll notice that all the chords use the same F bar chord shape, but each one goes one fret higher.

Move the fingers together as a block. You can go on and on like this up to the 10th, perhaps even 12th fret or higher in some guitars covering a full octave with major chords using a single shape.

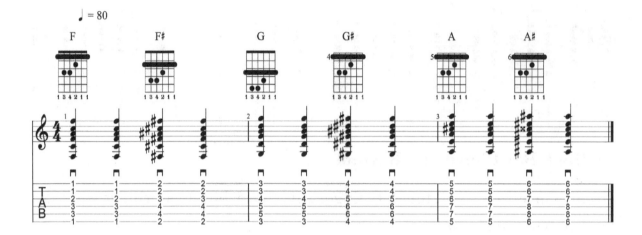

That's a wrap for now! It was a very productive session, right? Well, let's leave that index finger of yours to rest for a while before we tackle yet another important skill.

FAQ : How Can I Master a Chord I'm Stuck With?

When trying to play a chord that refuses to be played by you; don't try to get it to obey. Indeed, music is a beautiful thing that flows from your hands into the world. Because of that, the more you try, the more elusive that chord will get.

Instead, try leaving it for a while and come back to it with a fresh head and fresh hands. This approach works wonders; try it and you'll see the results.

Bar Chords on the 5th String

Just like we did in the power chord chapter, we're going to cover bar chords on the 5th string as well as on the 6th string. We're going to take the B chord as an example to show how these chords are made.

Also, just like we did before, we'll work our way there using simpler alternatives that will help us create a playable B major chord without the index creating the bar and we'll slowly put it all together.

Are you ready? Buckle up because here we go!

Half of the B Chord

This will be our first approach to this chord; a simplified, minimalist version of it.

Here we go:

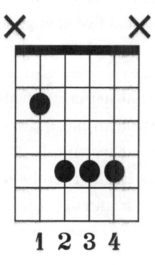

We don't play strings 1 nor 6 with this one. As in some other chords we've seen, you can use one or more fretting fingers to mute string 1 so that you don't have to worry about it when strumming.

Let's try this version of the B chord in a chord progression:

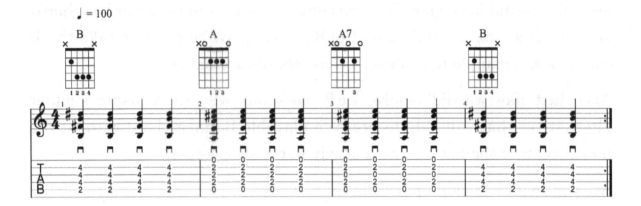

The Full B Bar Chord

Once the previous chord sounds well, it is time to use our index finger to create the full bar at the second fret and play the 2nd and 1st strings. Bear in mind that the chord doesn't include the 6th string so you should just strum the chord using the bottom five strings.

> **PRO TIP:** This is a tip that actually involves the tip of your index finger. Indeed, you can use it to mute the string immediately above by letting it touch it without fretting it. Moreover, since your finger will be slightly rolled, this might even be an involuntary thing. Pay attention to it and use it in your favor.

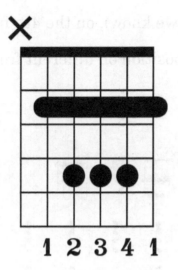

Here's the same progression above but with the full B bar chord.

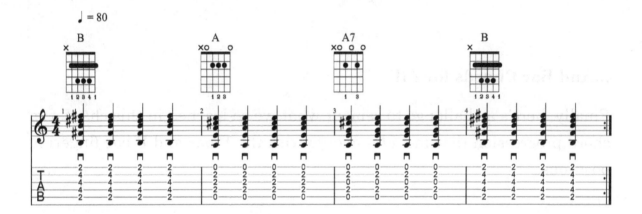

If you can't manage to make this one sound good, it's normal. All bar chords are hard at first. Until you learn it well, you can use the previous B chord we've learned.

To The B Bar Chord and Beyond

The B bar chord follows the same principle as the F chord in that once you can play it you can move it to other frets and get a lot of different chords. With the index on the 2nd fret, you get a B, on the 3rd fret a C (a bar C, different than the open C we know), on the 4th fret a C#/Db, and so on.

Let's try the B bar chord position on different frets:

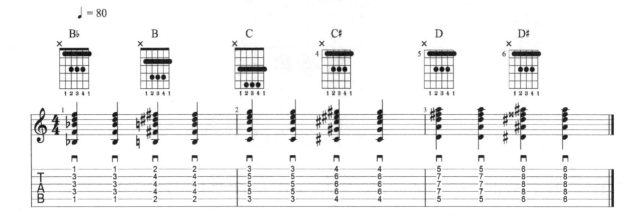

...And Bar Chords for All

Finally, here's a challenge to cement what we've learned in this chapter: a chord progression that includes chords with the F bar and B bar fingering positions.

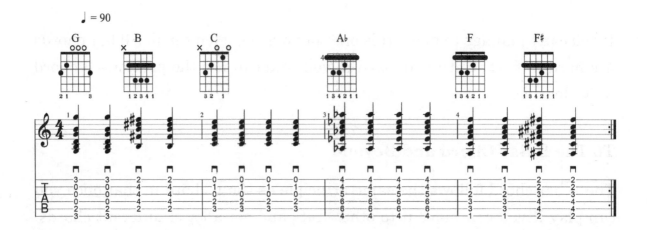

Conclusion

Congratulations on making it to the end of this book!

First of all, I would like to thank you for letting me be your guide on this journey to the heart and soul of guitar playing. I loved writing this book; I did it with all my heart, passion, and knowledge. I hope some of that got through to you and I inspired you to keep playing for a lifetime.

We've been through a journey of discovering the guitar... At neck-breaking speed!

In just a few days, you've discovered how to start playing the guitar, learned major chords, minor chords, seventh chords, major seventh chords, minor seventh chords, played various strumming patterns, experimented with arpeggios, tried using a capo, and learned how to play bar chords properly!

I'd say this book has been a great beginning for a successful and passionate career in guitar playing.

The guitar can transform into a lifelong companion that will be there for you during the hard times and can help you live experiences that challenge even your wildest dreams. But you're just warming up. Indeed, there is a lot to learn still to become the kind of guitar player you always envisioned to be.

Moreover, you achieved so much in less than a month that, with practice and more instruction, the world better be ready for your talent and tenacity!

"And now what?" You might be asking; well, the answer is very simple: just practice, practice, and practice some more until you've mastered every technique in this book. Then, go out and show the world what you can do with your six-string in your hands.

Moreover, if, at any point of this journey together, something picked your curiosity and you want to learn more about it, start with that and dig deeper.. The guitar is an infinite canvas and there is a vast ocean of knowledge ahead of you, ready to be explored.

Finally, make sure to check out the rest of our catalog, you can find more books like this that can work as a lighthouse pointing your efforts in the right direction.

Thank you again for letting me be a part of your guitar journey, I wish you the very best of luck, and may the guitar help you have fun, overcome difficult moments, and meet a lot of musician friends to share your passion with.

I hope to see you on stage somewhere helping others with your passion.

Happy guitar playing and have a wonderful life full of music and fun.

Farewell

Pssssttttt....

What are you doing here? Are you lost?

Do people even look at the last pages of a book?

Jokes aside, I hope you enjoyed this book. I certainly loved the process of writing it.

If you enjoyed this book, could you take 2 minutes to leave a review about it?

Reviews are the lifeblood for small publishers and help us get our books into the hands of more guitarists like you.

We read every review personally and appreciate each one of it.

To leave a review, simply go to the platform you purchased the book from and type in your review.

With that said, here's Guitar Head signing off!

Until next time then? I'll see you in another book.

The End

Made in United States
Troutdale, OR
12/07/2024

26010719R00091